RESCUE

RESCUE

THE HISTORY OF BRITAIN'S EMERGENCY SERVICES

BY
GAVIN WEIGHTMAN

B▦XTREE

IN ASSOCIATION WITH CHANNEL FOUR
TELEVISION CORPORATION

DEDICATION
This book is dedicated to the memory of Mike Dutfield

ACKNOWLEDGEMENTS
The inspiration for this book comes from Dr Ken Hines. A special thanks to him and to Wendy Neal, author of a book on Victorian disasters, who introduced me to Dr Hines. Neil Wallington was a mine of information on the postwar history of the fire service, and thanks to Judy Seaborne and Gordon White of the London Civil Defence and Fire Authority for their help. The Home Office were very helpful in giving their permission to quote from the CFBA Report No 6/92 'Detection Devices for Hidden or Buried Casualties'. For their personal memories and advice on many subjects thanks to Dr Ken Easton, Len Watson, Peter Simpson, Phil Arnold, and John Lawal. Rogan Taylor helped greatly with advice on the Hillsborough tragedy. At News International, Charlotte Brown went beyond the call of duty in her help with pictures for the book from that extensive library. Thanks to all the interviewees who have given their time, and to Tony Edwards, Nick Godwin, Edwina Cooper, Ann Walsh, Tim O'Connor, Clare Batty and David Hass for their work on the television series and Alison Kreps, Vanessa Frances and Thelma Rumsey for research for the book. At Boxtree, Katy Carrington has been an enthusiastic and very attentive editor without whose efforts this book would never have been finished on time. Finally, thanks to everyone at Barraclough Carey Productions for their support with the project, and to Peter Moore and Alan Hayling at Channel Four for commissioning the television series which this book accompanies.

First published in Great Britain in 1996 by Boxtree Limited

Text © Gavin Weightman 1996

The right of Gavin Weightman to be identified as Author of this Work has been asserted by him in accordance with the Copyright, Designs and Patents Act 1988.

1 3 5 7 9 10 8 6 4 2

Cover design by Slatter-Anderson
Designed by Design 23
Reprographics by Jade Reprographics, Braintree Essex
Printed and bound in Great Britain by Butler and Tanner, Frome, Somerset, for

Boxtree Limited
Broadwall House
21 Broadwall
London   SE1 9PL

A CIP catalogue entry for this book is available from the British Library.

ISBN 0 7522 1052 1

CONTENTS

INTRODUCTION

On the night of Sunday 8 January 1989, a Boeing 737 with 126 people on board crashed on the busy M1 motorway near Kegworth in Leicestershire. Within half an hour or so, the fire brigades, police, ambulance services and doctors of three counties had converged on the scene of the disaster. At one point there were 700 of them present, armed with an array of medicines, medical equipment and skills which would have amazed those who did the same kind of emergency work fifty years ago.

Take a step back in time to another disaster, the terrible rail crash that took place in October 1952 at Harrow and Wealdstone Station in Middlesex and you can see how far the rescue work of emergency services has advanced in half a century. At Harrow the services had no emergency plans in place to speak of, except those covering civil defence in time of war. Police toured the streets with loud-hailers, calling for doctors to come and help, and many turned up with little idea of what they were supposed to do. Ambulancemen then had no higher qualifications than a first-aid certificate, and in Middlesex, as in many other counties, the ambulance driver was a member of the fire brigade, though regarded as a lesser being than the noble firefighter.

Firemen themselves were still seen purely as brave 'smoke-eaters' and had barely any training or equipment to free people trapped in the wreckage of a train. The police at Harrow did their best, but they had little idea about how to contain the chaos at the scene, where the public swarmed unchallenged.

By contrast, at Kegworth in 1989 there were hospital flying squads, highly trained ambulancemen and women, whom we would now call paramedics; firefighters trained to cut people free from wreckage, their skills honed by the frequent extrication of motorists in road accidents; and police who by then had a concept of how order might be created from the confusion of a disaster scene.

It is impossible to say whether some of the 112 people who died in the Harrow crash would have been saved by the more sophisticated methods of modern rescue work: such assertions are not verifiable by scientific assessment. Nevertheless, it is obvious that between the 1950s and the present day there have been great advances in the work of the emergency services. We expect far more of firefighters (as firemen have been renamed since the mid-1980s), ambulancemen and women, doctors and police than we used to and take it for granted that at any accident or catastrophe our salaried Samaritans will be there in an instant with their state-of-the-art life-saving equipment to rescue as many people as humanly possible.

We might imagine that the improvements there have been over the past fifty years were simply the inevitable consequence of technological and medical 'progress'. In reality, however, practically none of them have been in any way pre-ordained or driven simply by scientific advances which made better, more effective and portable rescue equipment available. Developing the work of the emergency services has also been a continuous battle against entrenched ideas, medical prejudices, the natural conservatism of regimental organizations like the fire brigades, and strict financial controls. Above all, it was the initiative of a few individuals that brought about improvements.

In Britain, the first historical model for the emergency services was the Royal Humane Society, founded in 1774 to provide safety advice and rescue equipment for those who fell through the ice while skating or walking on frozen rivers and lakes. The society, a voluntary organization, set up 250 receiving houses next to London's waterways and lakes to provide emergency care. Ice men were supplied with hooks, ladders, boats, poles and other rescue equipment and 100 doctors, who were alerted by runners, gave their services free.

The ambulance service began as a voluntary movement in the nineteenth century, while the doctors dedicated to bringing medical care to the scene of accidents and disasters today are organized by a charitable body called BASICS – the British Association for Immediate Care. Since the Second World War, the fire brigades, too, have taken on a wide variety of rescue work which has nothing to do with firefighting, notably freeing motorists trapped in wreckage as a result of road accidents, for which they have neither a statutory responsibility nor extra funding.

Most of the strides which have been made have not come about in response to major disasters, for these are by their very nature relatively rare events determined by the scale of death and injury inflicted at one blow. It is through the more routine work of attending road accidents, saving those struck down by heart attacks or dealing with a host of minor mishaps that rescue workers have developed new skills. Since the war, each time a disaster has occurred there has been a little bit more knowledge, a little bit more in the way of pre-hospital care, a little bit more planning and co-ordination between the services.

To give a dramatic structure to the book, this account of the emergency services for the most part compares the response to an 'old' disaster (from the 1950s to the 1970s) with the way the services dealt with a more recent example. Thus the Harrow tragedy of 1952 is set against the Clapham train crash of 1988; road accidents in the 1950s are contrasted with a motorway pile-up in the 1990s; the Trident plane crash at Staines in 1972 with the Kegworth disaster in 1989; the wartime Blitz with the IRA bombing of the Grand Hotel,

Firemen take a break before going back underground to tackle the blaze at Smithfield Meat Market in 1958.

Brighton, in 1974; and the Moorgate tube catastrophe of 1975 with the Hillsborough football disaster of 1987.

Some of the incidents described, such as the road accidents of the 1960s, are not generally defined as disasters – there is in fact no agreed definition of the term. But what we take to be a disaster is an exceptionally large-scale accident or atrocity with a large number of casualties, and one which is usually remembered by the general public by a previously insignificant place name – Lockerbie, Moorgate, Hillsborough, for example. These are events which, because of their magnitude in terms of human suffering, make the headlines, and whose names hold a chilling resonance for us for ever afterwards.

For the emergency services, dealing with a disaster is something quite out of the ordinary, and many rescue workers will begin and end their careers without ever facing the special problems such catastrophes present. When a disaster does happen it is a tremendous shock to the system and exposes all kinds of weaknesses. It is, as one of those involved in the aftermath of the Kegworth air crash put it, like an ambush on the emergency services.

In recent years, planning for and rehearsing the response to possible disasters has become commonplace. As our emergency services are run locally rather than nationally, those who went to the rescue at Kegworth, say, may never have to go through such an experience again. The next time a plane comes down it might be in London rather than in Leicestershire, and dealing with it will be a totally new situation for nearly all of the local rescue workers. All the emergency services nationally now try to pass on to each other lessons learned locally, and master plans have been put in place incorporating this collective wisdom. Yet the universal experience of those who have had to face the real thing is that no amount of forethought can adequately prepare someone for a big plane or train crash. Master plans usually fall apart in the race to the rescue and in the adrenaline rush of those charged with saving the lives of a large number of badly injured people.

Although the response of local emergency services to a disaster will inevitably fall short of the planner's ideal, it is fair to say that in terms of the range of expertise and equipment brought to the scene, the handling of the next disaster will be an improvement on that of the last one. The most significant recent advance, for example, is the rise of the modern paramedic, the highly trained ambulanceman or woman of the 1990s. This is not to say that changes for the better are either continuous or inevitable, nor that the emergency services have little left to learn. On the whole, rescue workers receive public praise for their skills and gallantry with broad grins and like to pat themselves on the back for doing a good job, but privately they are fiercely self-critical, as much of the testimony in this book reveals.

Some of their stories are likely to strike the lay reader as shocking – a great deal of disaster work is gruesome in the extreme. Rescue workers seldom talk about it except among themselves, but here they give a rare insight into some of the realities they face. Their experiences should promote a greater understanding of the mistakes that are made and of the never-ending desire to 'do better next time'.

The choice of a particular incident to demonstrate a certain aspect of the work and development of the emergency services is arbitrary to a considerable extent: indeed, each of the disasters described in this book could be used to illustrate any of the themes explored. Consequently, only a part of each event can be focused upon here. The whole story of each disaster would require a book of its own. The two air crashes, for instance, have been taken together to highlight the advances made in controlling the chaos of the immediate aftermath of a disaster, and takes only a glance at the medical response. On the other hand, the comparison between Harrow and Clapham, used to show changes in the medical response to disasters, reveals little about the tremendous work of the firefighters who cut free trapped victims at Clapham. The story of how they got into the business of 'extrication' is told in Chapter Two.

In fact it is surprising how little firefighting has changed over the years, given the catalogue of new equipment a firefighter now has at his – or her – disposal. Essentially, battling against fire is still central to their work, and that is what excites them. Between the great Smithfield Meat Market fire of 1958 and the King's Cross disaster of 1987, the biggest change for the fire brigade has been the new hazards – especially toxic smoke – presented by the widespread use of plastics, synthetic materials and chemicals. This has necessitated a broadening of the skills in which firefighters are trained. They are also now the experts, not only in extricating victims of road accidents, but in rescuing people buried in the rubble of collapsed buildings. It is firefighters who carry and learn to use modern search equipment and who are expected to take on the most dangerous job they ever do: mining into the treacherous avalanche of masonry and brickwork to free those who are trapped alive.

The comparison of Moorgate and Hillsborough provides the horrific background to one of the most fiercely debated and contentious subjects in the emergency services today. How do rescue workers cope with the nightmare scenes they witness at a disaster? Just a glance at the London Fire Brigade's colour photographs of the grotesque remains of the Moorgate tube carriages that were rammed into a dead-end tunnel one morning would make any layman feel sick. Nowadays, rescue workers are often given counselling to help them get over their experiences. In 1975 hardly anybody gave this a thought. Whether or not there is such a thing as post-traumatic stress disorder, a condition from which rescue

The Revd John Richards who comforted victims trapped in the worst train disaster in postwar Britain at Harrow and Wealdstone station in 1952.

workers are likely to suffer and which requires treatment – and, in a few instances, financial compensation – is discussed by those who have been, or might be, affected: firefighters, policemen and women, ambulance workers, doctors and others.

It is an appropriate finale to the book, for it is the personal testimony of those who have gone to the rescue of others which provides the heart of this brief history. Their ability to cope calmly and efficiently with the most horrific circumstances is, in many instances, the essence of their heroism, as well as a mark of their professionalism. This history begins long before the psychological impact of rescue work was ever considered, on an autumn morning in 1952, when one of the worst railways disasters this century was about to happen.

CHAPTER ONE
THE VITAL HOUR

There was patchy fog on the morning of 8 October 1952 when the 7.31 train from Tring in Hertfordshire pulled out of the station and started on its way to Euston. Because the next train on this busy London commuter line had been cancelled, the 7.31 was carrying more coaches than usual – nine instead of the standard seven. By the time it reached Harrow and Wealdstone, seven minutes late, it was almost full.

The impatient commuters on the platform folded their newspapers and ran this way and that looking for a compartment with a free seat. This was the old kind of train you now see only in 1940s films or railway museums. There was no corridor and each compartment had its own door opening on to two bench-like seats set opposite each other. In theory, these could take six people each. All nine carriages on the

The incredible scene of rescuers in the wreckage of the Harrow and Wealdstone train disaster: if you look closely, you can pick out police and firemen among the hordes of unofficial helpers.

Tring train were third class, a Victorian social category retained by British Railways, the nationalized company created four years earlier by a triumphant Labour government.

Indeed, this local train, which prepared to leave Harrow and Wealdstone Station as the clock on the tower of the Victorian building showed 8.19am, was a microcosm of Britain in the 1950s. Both men and women were enjoying the return of peacetime clothing fashions now that the coupon system of rationing had been lifted. Many would have been among the crowds who, the year before, thronged the South Bank extravaganza of the Festival of Britain with its futuristic images and quite un-English modern buildings, of which the Festival Hall is the only relic. Earlier that year Britain had had an international triumph when the world's first jet passenger airliner, the Comet, went into service. Victorian ideas and values were fading and the death of George VI in February 1952 – his was the first royal funeral to be televised – marked the end of an era of bitter war and miserable austerity. The young queen, only twenty-six years old, seemed to promise a new Elizabethan age. She was due to be crowned the following June, and coronation fever had already begun.

Though modernism was in the air, the atmosphere and fabric of places like Harrow was still in many ways Victorian. This metroland had grown enormously between the wars as semi-detached suburbia was built, but it was still heated by coal fires and served by steam trains. In the Fifties, the future and the past were overlapping: the 'consumer society' was taking shape, thanks to the modest postwar affluence that inspired the ageing Prime Minister, Harold Macmillan, to proclaim by 1957, 'Let's face it, some of us have never had it so good.'

On the morning of 8 October, the autumn mist was thickened by the coal smoke which had risen from thousands of chimneys the night before as the first fires were lit to take the chill off suburban living rooms. There was smoke too from factories, and great puffs of sooty steam were flung across the platforms of Harrow and Wealdstone Station by the express trains which rattled its nineteenth-century foundations as they raced northwards or on the way 'up' – as they still said in railway parlance – to Euston. The commuters now pulling closed the doors of the Tring train were immune to the sound of these express trains approaching. Every morning they shot by with their deafening clatter, dislodging hats and rustling newspapers in their moist slipstream. Every morning 100 potential disasters were averted by the man in the signal box who directed both local and express trains as they criss-crossed the fast and the slow lines. With an elaborate pulling of levers and ringing of bells, the signalman worked within well-tried safety margins, always watching from the windows of the signal box, peering through the mist at the shimmering lines glistening silver in the morning mist.

It took a while for all the people waiting at Harrow and Wealdstone to find a place on the train. Clutching their lunch packs, they squeezed in where they could, some having to stand wedged between the knees of those sitting facing each other. Many who customarily got in at the back ran towards the centre of the train in search of a seat. In theory, the seventy-four compartments should have provided a seat for all 800 or so people now on the train, but, as every commuter knows, the distribution of passengers is never perfect, and on a train without corridors it was bound to be uneven. To ease the congestion, the guard, flag and whistle at the ready, had even allowed some passengers into his brake van, the seventh carriage. He walked briskly to the rear of the train, shutting doors on packed compartments in which many people were strap-hanging and shuffling their feet to find a comfortable position. The last two carriages, the extra ones, were old, made of wood on a steel frame way back in 1916 and 1921.

As the brakes were released, and the passengers felt the first jolt with relief that they were on their way, the guard, about to skip back into the brake van, turned in alarm. Bearing down on the back of his train was an enormous express. He leaped across to the far side of the platform and jumped down on to the line. There was an almighty crash, so loud it deafened him. He peeked over the edge of the platform and saw that the rear coaches had been virtually turned to matchwood; to all intents and purposes they had disappeared. The Perth to London sleeper had ridden right over the Tring train and was wedged on its side under the now half-demolished road bridge which crossed the line near the station. Moments later there was another explosion of sound as the London to Liverpool express, pulled by a 'double-header' – two engines weighing hundreds of tons – and travelling at around 60mph, came under the road bridge and hit the wreckage of the first express. It flew in the air, landing on its side near the front of the Tring train.

No individual can, at the moment such a catastrophe happens, take in more than a fraction of the scene. The signalman had known it was going to happen because he had seen the southbound express race past his box. He had instantly tried to stop the northbound Liverpool train but he was just too late – the driver had passed the signal just before it switched to 'danger'. Somehow on that misty morning the driver of the Perth sleeper had misread a signal, perhaps because of the tricks of light that could occur as the sun broke through the haze. The exact cause would remain a mystery, for the driver was now entombed in the wreckage of his engine.

At first none of the passengers on the Tring train knew what had happened. One of them, Evelyn Hargood, still has a vivid memory of the confusion in her carriage.

She and her husband had been standing when the train was hit.

My first impression was that it was very jerky. As the train went forward I knocked a man's hat off, and I remember saying, 'Oh, I am sorry,' and just as I said that the

There were many helping hands for this victim of the Harrow crash, but precious little in the way of emergency medicine.

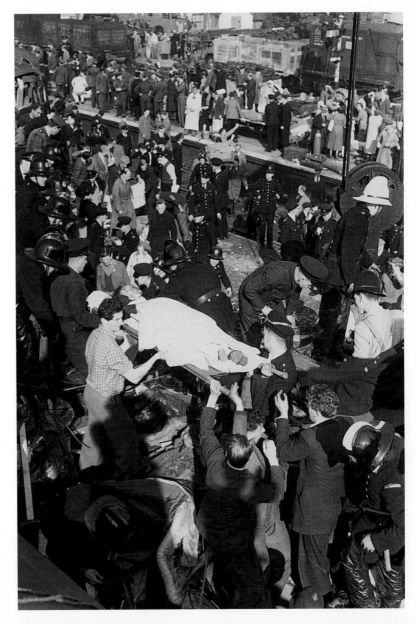

whole train bolted forward. We had been strap-hanging, and I remember holding on for as long as possible. Then I clung on to the luggage rack, which was made out of fishing net-type material, and I just hung on until I could not hold it any longer. It was dark and dusty and there was a tremendous smell of sulphur from one of the other trains. I was groping in the dark trying to find my husband. I found his hand. I could not see, but I knew it was him.

He pulled me up from the tangle of legs and arms. All these people around us were groaning and moaning with pain. I was wearing high-heeled shoes and I remember thinking, 'I hope I am not standing on someone's face.' A lot of people were badly hurt but nobody panicked. People were saying, 'Get off my face!' Although it was dark in the carriage there was enough light for me to see this poor man bleeding. I took his telephone number and later phoned his wife to let her know that he was OK. He had a broken pelvis. There were shoes and bags lying everywhere. People used to bring their lunches to work, and the carriage was full of sandwiches and apples.

We were thinking about air. Somebody had a pen-knife so he cut through a leather strap holding a window shut. When we got it open a little, people outside told us to climb out. We helped others through and my husband and I were the last out. I don't remember the ambulance people being there. Lots of people were screaming and crying and we just wanted to get away. For three nights afterwards we could hear the oxyacetylene cutters, and in a way that was the worst thing, because I realized they must still be cutting out people who were trapped.

From the many descriptions people have given of the Harrow disaster it is clear that the rescue operation, though it was mounted swiftly enough, bore very little resemblance to the highly organized and professional response of emergency services today. This was especially true of the emergency medical care, the work of doctors and ambulancemen. Officially, as well as the 112 people killed, 157 were taken to hospital, where 84 were detained, and 183 had other injuries. Presumably Mrs Hargood and her husband, and other survivors with minor injuries, were not counted. Many got the bus home without ever reporting to police at the scene that they were among the victims. One of them, Arthur Collyer, was in the third carriage from the back.

There was a hell of a crash and an awful sound of metal splintering as our coach was pushed up in the air and right over. I was knocked un-conscious. When I came to I could see the area was a complete shambles. I lost all my belongings. All around me was solid metal. As I came round, somebody must have been lifting metal off my leg, because I felt some pain and shouted, 'Get off my leg.' I could just see a small chink of light and I crawled through a tiny gap. I saw a friend and I said, 'Come on, you can't stay here,' but he told me his legs were broken. I tried to help, but I kept thinking 'What can I do?'.

Mr Collyer, even though he had been unconscious, took a bus back to Watford, where he presented himself at a local hospital three hours after the crash. He says they had still not heard about it, even though this must have been around 11am.

Some idea of the haphazard nature of the rescue operation and the degree to which the emergency services of the time were ill equipped to deal with it is provided by Peter Bloomfield, a coach driver now in semi-retirement. In 1952 he was in the RAF, based at nearby Stanmore. He was then a driving instructor and was taking a truck with some airmen in the back through Harrow. There was a hold-up as he neared the scene of the crash and a policeman approached him.

He asked if I was doing anything important. I said I wasn't, and he told me about the crash and asked if I could help. I was asked to post two men at a gate to keep sightseers out and then to help the firemen get people out of the wreckage.

It was chaos. I was trying to find bodies – we were searching through the rubble, saying, 'Here's one, this one is dead.' There was a compartment with people sitting opposite each other. It had collapsed inwards and these people were sandwiched together. The fire brigade had cut through the top of the carriage and all you could see was their hair. They needed a short, slight person to crawl down inside. I am 5ft 7in so they asked me. There was an American airman who had been sitting opposite a young lady. He was pushed so tight against her that his left ear left a perfect impression on her cheek. We dragged out dozens of people who were still alive.

Judged by modern standards, the heroic rescue work at Harrow was not much more than a chaotic rush to comfort the injured and pack those who could be stretchered out – often on detached train doors – into ambulances equipped merely with a first-aid kit, and whose drivers could perform little or nothing in the way of life-saving pre-hospital treatment. Yet for the period there was nothing especially bad about the rescue services at Harrow: in the immediate postwar years there was nowhere else in Britain with a more sophisticated system. The accepted practice was to get badly injured survivors of a disaster to hospital as quickly as possible so that they could be given specialist treatment there. Although in wartime the military medics had

recognized the value of giving the injured some basic life-saving treatment before they got to hospital, this concept had not yet found favour in the response to civilian accidents and disasters. The view was that if a hospital was nearby, the quicker the casualties were taken there the better.

This was understandable, because the range of drugs and equipment that doctors and ambulancemen could take to the scene of a disaster was very limited. Until the early 1960s, when some sections of medical opinion began to voice the view that whisking the injured off to hospital might do them more harm than good, and that it was better to give some treatment on the spot, there was no reason to develop the necessary equipment, or to train anybody to use it. The campaign to

Firemen help carry a casualty to waiting ambulances at Harrow. In the 1950s, the ambulance service was administered by the fire brigades.

improve the response of all the emergency services to accidents and disasters was therefore led by doctors, who argued that hospital care was of no benefit to the many survivors of accidents who died before they got there. During this critical period between injury and treatment (later termed the 'golden hour' by those who dealt with casualties in the Vietnam War), lives could be saved, the doctors said, by a sophisticated form of first aid which was to become known as pre-hospital or immediate care.

It was essentially an argument for applying a military model of emergency care to civilian disasters, a central feature of which was the practice of sorting out the casualties and labelling them according to the severity of their injuries and their chances of survival. Those who were dead or clearly about to die could be left to one side to allow the rescuers to concentrate on those it was still possible to save.

For this procedure to work, a clearing station has to be set up for what is called 'triage'. The word is derived from the French verb *trier*, which means to sort out. It was probably first used to describe the classification of casualties by Napoleon's chief medical officer, Baron Dominique-Jean Larry. His practice was to give priority to those soldiers who were capable of going back into the fray after medical treatment. Those who could not be patched up were left until later.

At a disaster like Harrow, triage would have involved a rapid assessment of the casualties by doctors at the scene, who would have labelled the victims using a colour-coding system. Those requiring immediate medical care if they were to survive would have been given priority, those not about to die, but still in need of urgent medical attention, would have formed a second category and the walking wounded a third. Those already dead or who could not be saved would have been a fourth group. Even very recently the triage of casualties at disasters has presented serious problems because different hospitals and ambulance services use different

systems of classification. Only in the mid-1990s has it has been agreed that red should indicate top priority, yellow the second level, green the walking wounded and black those who are dead.

Nowadays there is a great variety of triage labels which carry information about a casualty's general condition, details of treatment he or she has been given on site and the nature of his or her injuries. For patients arriving at hospital after the Harrow disaster, there were few records of what painkillers they had been given or even whether they had been persuaded to drink a cup of tea. As there was no triage or clearing station there was no information at the scene of the disaster that could be relayed to the hospitals taking in the casualties.

The atmosphere at Harrow in the first few minutes after the crash is remembered vividly by Bob Darvell, who was one of the first Middlesex ambulancemen on the scene. He joined the service in 1951, when the qualifications required were passing a driving test and a medical. He was also told to get a first-aid certificate, which would mean a pay rise.

We approached the station from the back and pulled into the goods yard. It was a shock: bedlam, chaos – it upsets me to remember it. I had never seen anything like it. As we arrived we were inundated with injured people crying, 'Help!' We opened the back of the ambulance and it was swamped. People were just loading the injured on, some of them on train seats – one person tried to load a casualty who was on a train door, but it wouldn't fit!

People were bleeding and screaming. We were overwhelmed, there was no way we knew where to start, and in those days our equipment was minimal – we had a first-aid box and bandages. People were just grabbing the bandages – there was no organization. Eventually we set off with five casualties, all seriously injured, two on stretchers and one on the floor.

Bob Darvell took the injured to Edgware Hospital in an ambulance which had no radio.

When he had dropped off his casualties he had to find a phone to contact the ambulance control and say that he was available again. He went back to the scene, where the rescue work was still going on and more ambulances and doctors had turned up. But the medical response remained patchy.

Dr Joseph Lister was at Harrow Hospital, getting changed to play tennis, when he got a call asking him if he was available to go to the scene of the disaster.

I took my bag with some injections, and went to the local chemist on the way, not knowing how much I would need. When I got to the station, I said to myself, 'Where the hell do I start?' Everybody was rushing around but after an hour or so it settled down a bit. I was told by someone wearing gold braid to go and join a group helping on the express train. I was working in the wreckage, mostly among the iron girders and the dust. I was not pulling people out, I was treating them. People were saying, 'How about this one, Doc? What about this guy?'

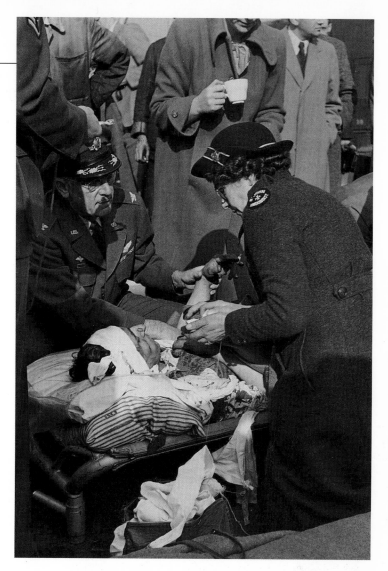

Many Harrow victims were given hot, sweet tea to comfort them which caused problems for hospital doctors if they later needed to administer a general anaesthetic.

As it turned out, Dr Lister eventually found himself in an emergency medical team which was much better equipped than the local ambulance crews or any of the family or hospital doctors who arrived from nearby. An hour after the crash, as policemen toured the district with loud-hailers appealing for doctors to come forward, a call was put out to nearby American Air Force bases to send in medical teams. There was still a great deal of rescue work to be done when they arrived at about 10.30am, two hours after the crash.

Dr Lister remembers: 'The Americans had everything: blood plasma drips – they were performing operations on site.' In contrast to the local ambulance crews, the Americans had state-of-the-art emergency medicines and sufficient skills to begin to treat patients while they were still trapped in the wreckage. There was official commendation for the work of the Americans, who were said to have saved the lives of twelve people, and the newspapers of the day paid tribute to 'the Yanks'. A black nurse, Abbie Sweetvine, briefly became a heroine when her picture was published in the national press.

RESCUE

Local ambulancemen, too, were greatly impressed by the skills and equipment of the Americans. John Moss joined the ambulance service just after the war. He had wanted to be a policeman, but the force turned him down and suggested he tried the fire brigade. They said he was too small, and recommended that he built up his muscles by working as an ambulanceman. In the end, he remained in the ambulance service for thirty-eight years. He was stationed at Friern Barnet, and did not attend the crash scene until the second day. Even at that late stage, he feels, the operation was still badly organized.

This was the incident that taught us we

Lt Abbie Sweetvine was in one of the medical teams from nearby American Air Force bases who brought the only really effective emergency medicine to the disaster.

could not handle disasters. We had no plan and no way of treating people at the scene. First-aid training consisted of eight one-hour lectures which took place on the job, but really, you learned by your mistakes. Our chief took a convoy of ambulances down to the scene and they just picked up the first people they found and took them to hospital. This filled up the vehicles and beds with people who weren't necessarily the worst cases. We were pulling out doctors from the hospitals to which we were taking patients, so there were none left to treat them when they got there.

The Americans made our eyes pop out with all their organization and equipment. It was just after the war, and our guys were very impressed. It was the only time I have been at an accident where you had coffee and cigarettes the whole time.

While the Americans had coffee and cigarettes, the Women's Royal Voluntary Service (WRVS) had tea and sympathy, a service they still provide at modern disasters. The St John Ambulance, in their familiar white sashes, were there, too. Many of these pioneer ambulancemen arrived not in ambulances, but by the first bus they could catch.

What might be called the official assessment of the emergency care can be found in the columns of the two great medical journals, the *Lancet* and the *British Medical Journal*. Both carried a letter from J. W. Watkins, chief regional officer of the London Midland Region, which read:

As I have been unable to obtain a complete list of all the doctors who rendered aid to those injured in the unfortunate train accident at Harrow and Wealdstone on October 8, I should be grateful for the opportunity to send my sincere thanks to all of them through the medium of your Journal.

I know the names of some of them, of course, whilst others preferred to remain anonymous, but in keeping with the highest traditions of the medical profession all of them rendered such invaluable aid that it is impossible to estimate how many more lives would have been so tragically lost had it not been for the medical attention given to them either before or immediately after they were brought from the wreckage.

I should like each and every doctor concerned to accept my very sincere and grateful thanks.

The fact that there was no record of the doctors at Harrow is itself symptomatic of the lack of a coherent plan of action, and indeed there were critical voices among doctors themselves in the same issue of the *British Medical Journal* (25 October 1952) in which Mr Watkins' letter of thanks was published. The most forthright came from R. Tudor-Edwards, a former St John Ambulance surgeon who had been in charge of the local mobile unit during the Blitz, and who perceptively contrasted American efficiency with the potentially fatal procedures of the well-meaning local doctors.

The accident took place at 8.20am on a fine and dry day, and so conditions were fortunate for first aid. An outstanding episode was the arrival of the American Air Force orderlies and nurses. They rendered most efficient first aid and also gave intravenous plasma transfusion on the spot. What was most important, every casualty went away properly labelled and marked to the awaiting ambulances.

The local doctors did pioneer work. They climbed through the wreckage to the trapped victims, and large numbers of victims were given morphine injections, but once released they were whisked away so quickly that it was almost impossible to designate what treatment they had received. I endeavoured to give the trapped victims drinks of bicarbonate of soda (two teaspoonfuls to the pint of water), but without exception those who were able to drink absolutely refused to take more than a feeding-cupful.

Naturally, enormous numbers of uniformed personnel were very soon on the spot – railwaymen, firemen, policemen and, to begin with, a few Red Cross and St John Ambulance men and officers. There was a sea of blue or dark blue uniforms, and it occurred to me that so far as medical personnel were concerned the blue and bluish uniforms should be discarded and a new uniform of very distinctive colour introduced . . .

There is no doubt that the services would be able to supply a first-aid field unit like the American one, to proceed at short notice to anywhere in the country.

The second censorious letter in the *Journal* came from two doctors at Edgware General Hospital who cared for survivors of the crash. They pointed out that of the fifty-four patients they kept in for observation on the wards, they believed thirteen had received morphine injections, but there was no information about their medication, and some victims had no idea what they had been given. Some had clearly had more than one injection. There were cases where people who were thought to have been unconscious from the crash had in fact been pole-axed by too much morphine. The doctors cast doubt on the wisdom of administering fluids at the scene and thought it best to get the victims to hospital as quickly as possible. And they did not approve of the rafts of hot, sweet tea that had been given to the badly injured as this was likely to make them vomit and worsen their condition if they subsequently needed a general anaesthetic.

The *BMJ* editorial assured its readers:

It was in no sense of carping criticism, therefore, that the two letters were written which appear in our correspondence columns this week. After every such emergency it is wise to review the procedure adopted in bringing first aid to the injured and to search thoroughly for any, even the slightest weakness, in the arrangements provided.

It seemed almost as if the *Journal* was a little embarrassed to carry any criticism when such heroic work had been done.

The leader referred to the American Air Force, which 'rendered such signal service to the wounded', but avoided unfavourable comparisons with the local medical response. While doffing its hat to the Americans, it concluded that the recently disbanded wartime mobile medical teams that had tended the wounded in the Blitz might not be cost-effective in peacetime. Perhaps, it was suggested, a skeleton service could be retained in case of another war.

Despite these little difficulties, the informed medical opinion was that everyone had done a splendid job. The *Lancet* felt no need to applaud the Americans (no mention is made of them in the editorial of 6 December), but suggested that perhaps the Royal Air Force mobile medical units could be useful in future. There should be a 'medical incident officer', it reasoned, to oversee the work of doctors (there had been none at Harrow) and every hospital should have plans to deal with major incidents. But, generally speaking, 'the less that is done before the injured reach hospital, the better'.

However, in the *Daily Telegraph*, under the headline: 'FIRST AID FOR RAIL VICTIMS – PREPARING A PLAN IN ADVANCE', there was the dissenting voice of a Dr N. P. Jewell, who went to the scene of the crash and was not at all impressed by the medical response. He wrote:

Sir,

I would like to draw attention to some aspects of the recent railway disaster at Harrow and to suggest that some form of medical procedure should be worked out as a precaution in the event of future catastrophes.

In response to a call I was present at the station very shortly after the smash. I found, as one might expect, a chaotic state of affairs. The fire services were trying to prevent the wreckage taking fire. Large numbers of police were present and there were swarms of civilians, some engaged in rescue work but the majority just looking on.

Most of the many doctors were wondering what to do as no dressing station had been set up. The system was to call a doctor to administer morphia as soon as the casualty could be reached. There were no medical supplies to be seen. Later, an American unit opened up a dressing station with full equipment and did very fine work.

The first thing, in my opinion, should be to clear the area of all persons not engaged in the work of rescue and to keep it clear by police cordon. Secondly, a dressing station should be set up.

Thirdly, every railway station should have emergency medical equipment available on the spot. This should include casualty labels to be attached to each individual treated, with a record of all treatment given – especially morphia injections – to prevent several injections being unwittingly administered to the same casualty.

Fourthly, every hospital should have an emergency team ready to leave at short notice with sterilizers, blood-transfusion apparatus, bandages, spare labels etc.

These simple measures would bring order out of chaos. Surely when an accident occurs in the middle of a populous area, with hospitals within easy reach and plenty of ambulances available, it should not be necessary for civilians to tear up their sheets for bandages, and wait until our American friends bring equipment to help us.

It was still common in the 1950s to describe the kind of treatment the medical and emergency services could bring to a disaster as 'first aid'. To most people today, that term would be interpreted as the most rudimentary form of medical assistance, which members of the public can learn if they wish. It has to do with techniques of bandaging, of mouth-to-mouth resuscitation (an innovation of the 1960s), of wrapping the injured up so that they look like Egyptian mummies. What doctors at Harrow called first aid evolved over the years into the kind of on-the-spot treatment which became known as 'immediate care'. This falls between first aid and the sophisticated, hospital-based treatment of traumatic injury. It is a means of saving life long enough for the magicians of modern medicine to work miracles on the victims of misfortune.

In those days the therapeutic and life-saving potential of 'first aid' was not taken seriously, but once it developed into 'immediate care' it could be applied to the noisy and distracting atmosphere of a disaster. Whereas the hospital doctor knows how to perform in an operating theatre, his colleague trained to give treatment at the scene of a disaster can, with specialist equipment, save the life of someone buried alive in the horribly contorted wreckage of a train, plane or motor car.

Those rescue workers who find themselves in the midst of a catastrophe like the Harrow crash have to ask themselves if it is better to get a victim out as fast as possible, however dreadful his or her condition, and off to hospital in an ambulance, or to work as fast as

they can there and then to prevent the victim's condition from getting any worse. Clearly, in 1952, the British medical view was 'scoop and run' – never mind the pulse rate, get the patient professional hospital treatment as soon as possible. The Americans, however, following a military tradition evolved on the battlefield, had more confidence in their immediate care: they would 'stay and stabilize' the casualty before handing him or her on to the more sophisticated attentions of the hospital.

The question of whether it is best to 'scoop and run' or 'stay and stabilize' remains at the heart of a controversy which has a long history in the evolution of the emergency services. It is

Local women roll bandages for the Harrow injured, made from their torn-up sheets. A touching illustration of the rescue work of the time – heartfelt, but amateur.

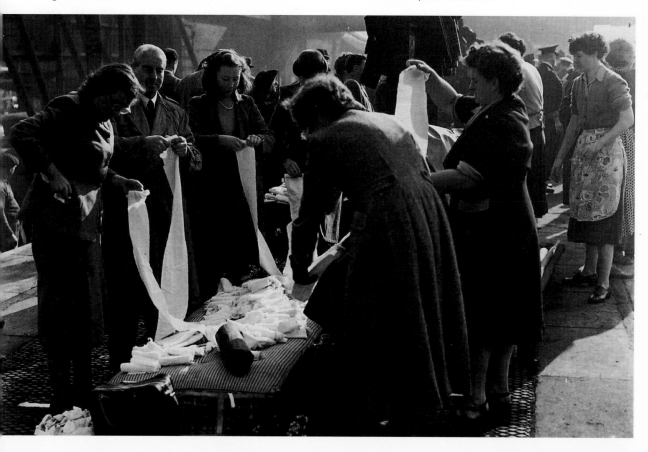

a debate which continues as the portable equipment ambulancemen and doctors can take to the scene of an accident or disaster becomes more and more advanced. The role and training of the ambulance service is critical to this issue, for their people will nearly always be at the scene of a disaster before any doctors.

Peacetime disasters which leave large numbers of people injured and dying have always presented a scene reminiscent of the urgency and chaos of the battlefield, and indeed it was in warfare that the idea of an ambulance service evolved. Baron Dominique-Jean Larry, the French military surgeon who developed triage, also invented the first 'ambulance volante' during the Napoleonic Wars at the end of the eighteenth century. His prototypes were simply stretchers on wheels which were used to get wounded soldiers from the battlefield to a hospital centre where their injuries could be treated. The idea of using the same sort of ambulance to help the victims of peacetime accidents on the railways or in industry caught on during the nineteenth century, especially as a result of the terrible carnage of the American Civil War of the 1860s. In fact, the very first civilian ambulance services were started in America in the years just after the end of the Civil War. A Union Army surgeon, Edward B. Dalton, set up New York City's first service in 1865. Whereas the military ambulances carried as many wounded as possible, the civilian versions – crudely adapted wagons with blankets, a mattress and a few bits of first-aid equipment – carried fewer patients.

Britain had no ambulance services at all at that time, but in the 1870s a great 'ambulance movement' began. It was concerned not only with the concept of adapting battlefield ambulances for use in towns and industrial areas, but with teaching 'first aid' to as wide a range of people as possible. Leading this campaign in Britain was the St John Ambulance Association, founded in 1877. Its leading lights had set up the British National Society for the Sick and Wounded during the Franco–Prussian war of 1870, and had become familiar with ambulance design and with what they called 'first aid', a term first coined in 1879 from a combination of 'first treatment' and the popular nickname for the society, 'National Aid'.

The St John Ambulance Association began to set up ambulance services in the mining areas of the north of England where terrible accidents seriously injured thousands every year. All the old heavy industries were dangerous, and in the Potteries, the steel towns and eventually on the railways, the work of the St John campaigners laid the foundation for the modern ambulance service. They produced ambulance textbooks, awarded certificates in first aid and trained workers in dangerous industries. They also began to train the police and the fire service in first aid, and in fact some of the early ambulance services in towns were run by the police or the fire brigade.

Odd though it might seem, it took a long while for this innovation to be accepted. St John Ambulance brigades, with their distinctive black and white uniforms, were often tainted with cries of 'Bodysnatchers!' in the early days. A breakthrough came with Queen Victoria's Golden Jubilee celebrations of 1887, when the St John volunteers first took on the task of attending major events, something they still do today.

The ambulance services, then, are the newest of our emergency services. They were for a very long time entirely voluntary and they have been attached to both the police and the fire brigade. In fact, it was not until the creation of the National Health Service in 1948 – only four years before the Harrow crash – that local authorities were bound to provide ambulance services, and even then they could simply hire the St John Ambulance as their agents. There were local authority services before that, some of them, like the London Ambulance Service, quite well equipped for their time, but nothing like what we have today. It was not until 1974 that ambulances were run by health authorities.

Indeed, at the time of the Harrow crash all the emergency services were very different from their contemporary versions. The fire brigade was there chiefly to put out fires – they did not provide general rescue assistance. The ambulancemen, as described earlier, were very much the poor relations of the firefighters. One of the ambulancemen who attended Harrow, John Moss, confirms how lowly their position could be when they were run as part of the fire service. 'The ambulance service was very much looked down upon by the fire brigade – we were regarded as their lesser cousins. They would often get us to peel their spuds and wash their floors.'

It was not long after the Harrow crash – and partly as a result of that experience – that a movement began which bore some resemblance to the St John Ambulance campaigns nearly a century earlier. It was pioneered by doctors, mostly general practitioners, who, from the mid-1950s, found themselves faced with a new and gruesome pandemic: the death toll on the roads. The volume of traffic was nothing like as heavy as it is today, of course, but nonetheless the number of accidents had become a national scandal. Very often crashes happened ten or fifteen miles from the nearest hospital, and those who were called to them – usually family doctors with practices close by – felt powerless to help.

One of these doctors was Kenneth Easton, who had worked in London during the Blitz and had been a member of one of the medical teams which helped survivors of the concentration camps at the end of the war. He went to Catterick in Yorkshire in 1949 first as a medical officer to the RAF depot there. Working close to the A1, he was regularly called out to accidents, along with RAF nurses, who became known in the popular press as 'angels of the A1'. Time after time, Dr Easton found severely injured victims of road crashes trapped in their cars or lorries with little chance of surviving the crude efforts to get them out and a long ride to hospital with minimal first aid. His tireless campaigning led to the formation of the pioneer Road Accident After Care Scheme, which first went into action in

1967. This inspired other similar schemes.

This development was not confined to Britain: in Germany the medical problems of dealing with road accidents was also recognized in the 1960s, and through correspondence and conferences, a kind of international expertise was built up. Professor Eberhard Gogler of Heidelberg University coined the term 'therapeutic vacuum' at this time to describe the period in which accident victims were pulled from the wreckage and taken to hospital. To fill that vacuum, Gogler and a team from the university surgical unit successfully pioneered a scheme whereby they equipped themselves to carry out a form of immediate care which involved keeping victims' airways clear, replacing lost blood and fluids, providing anaesthetics, and making sure that before they were moved, casualties were in a stable condition.

Other British schemes included Bath's Accident Flying Squad, which was set up as early as 1961 by Roger Snook, a consultant in accident and emergency medicine at the Royal United Hospital. The squad was not attached to the hospital: Snook made Bath Fire Brigade and Ambulance Service the centre of operations. This flying squad assembled its own equipment, choosing what it could find that was suitable for swift action at the roadside. Some of it was quite folksy: the doctors' safety jackets were home-made from upholstery material and had reflective strips and lettering sewn on. But they were a vital piece of equipment in the days when rescuers were routinely mown down by passing motorists.

The doctors who came to specialize in emergencies were always on the lookout for new pieces of medical equipment, for the best kind of anaesthetic to use at the scene of an accident, and anxious that other services – the fire brigade and ambulancemen – should be better equipped and trained. This novel approach was to give the fire brigade an entirely new role in dealing with accidents and disasters, a subject which will be explored in detail in Chapter Two.

The Road Accident After Care Schemes grew steadily from 1967, but they never provided cover for more than about a quarter of the country. In 1977 a new organization emerged. BASICS – the British Association for Immediate Care – brought together all the initiatives that had been taken to improve the knowhow and techniques of doctors, still mostly GPs, who volunteered for accident work. There are now around 2,000 such doctors in Britain. Most take special training courses on treating badly injured patients. Firefighters teach them about the use of breathing apparatus, and the police give them instruction in how to drive fast and safely to an incident. To assist them they now have specially equipped cars with flashing lights.

As might be expected, BASICS schemes are committed to the idea that the old 'scoop and run' approach is often inappropriate at accidents and disasters. To fill the 'therapeutic vacuum', the doctors very often need the assistance of ambulance workers who have more than a few hours of first aid training. The organization has therefore campaigned for advanced training for ambulancemen and women in resuscitation techniques and it is largely through their efforts that the first paramedics began to appear in Britain in the 1990s.

It was not only BASICS doctors who were keen to have better trained ambulancemen and women. An increasingly common problem, and one to which the idea of a 'therapeutic vacuum' was very relevant, was that many people who suffered heart attacks died on their way to hospital. Special 'coronary ambulances' with the necessary equipment for keeping a patient alive might save many, but such mobile cardiac units were expensive and, like the road accident mobile operating theatres tried in some areas in the 1960s, they remained more an ambition than a reality in terms of widespread use. And they were worthless unless the crews were trained in the use of the equipment.

Dr Douglas Chamberlain, a consultant cardiologist at Brighton General Hospital in the early 1970s, was convinced that such specially equipped and staffed ambulances were a good idea, but at first he could not raise the funds to get such a service off the ground. His hospital did possess one 'coronary ambulance', but it could only be manned by an ordinary crew; consequently, its value was limited and it was rarely used. A single incident made Dr Chamberlain redouble his campaign until he convinced his hospital of the necessity for proper provisions. Like many cardiologists, Dr Chamberlain would routinely visit his patients at home. On one such call a patient suffered a severe heart attack. As Dr Chamberlain attempted to revive him with mouth-to-mouth resuscitation and chest compression he decided to call for the underused 'coronary ambulance' back at the hospital.

I told the patient's wife to immediately dial 999 and ask for the ambulance with the defibrillator [a machine for kick-starting the heart]. Eventually an ambulance did arrive, but it wasn't the right one! The driver casually announced that he'd been asked to survey the scene to see if sending out the coronary ambulance was really necessary, as it would involve finding a doctor capable of using the equipment. Becoming increasingly frustrated and angry at the amount of time being wasted, I explained that I was a cardiologist and so there was no need to find anyone else. I sent him off with instructions not to return unless he had the machine. Meanwhile the patient was still viable, but time was running out.

The coronary ambulance eventually arrived, manned by another doctor. He then proceeded to bring various bits and pieces of equipment into the house, leaving the one thing I really needed – the defibrillator – until last. When I eventually plugged it in, the damn thing exploded, with smoke and dust going everywhere. The whole thing was just like a scene out of a black comedy. By this time the poor patient was beyond revival and his wife started to sob hysterically while the other doctor and I got involved in a huge slanging match. When the dust settled – literally – and we'd run out of harsh words, I realized that a situation like this should never be allowed to happen again. The solution seemed obvious: if ambulance staff were trained to use defibrillators and maybe acquired other advanced skills, then certain patients' chances of survival would be improved.

There was great resistance to Chamberlain's plan. He was told that ambulance crews were 'like monkeys – you can teach them up to three tricks and not much more'. However, his persistence paid off and he was allowed to run an experimental scheme. Crew members were chosen and trained up, and they soon began to demonstrate that they could be taught many more 'tricks' if encouraged to do so.

The Brighton advanced training scheme was quickly taken up in one or two more places, but the medical profession in general remained largely opposed to it and the Department of Health was sceptical. It was not until the early 1980s that official backing and some government funding was given for the training of what we now call paramedics.

BASICS doctors and better-trained ambulance crews refined their skills, equipment and experience by dealing with a steady flow of day-to-day road accidents, heart-attack emergencies and other routine incidents. The time would come when their skills would be put to the ultimate test – a disaster. Because it was so well covered by the newsreels of the day, the Harrow crash of 1952 was used as a kind of training video – on how *not* to go about it.

When Dr Ken Hines first saw the wreckage of the train crash at Clapham on the morning of

An aerial view of the Clapham rail crash of 1988, in which an express hit a packed local commuter train and a third train ploughed into the wreckage.

12 October 1988 he was reminded of Harrow. Three trains had careered into each other. The 7.18am from Basingstoke had stopped on its way into Clapham Junction. On the same line, running just behind, was the 6.14 from Poole, and coming out of Clapham Junction was the 8.03 to Haslemere, which should have passed the first two trains on an adjoining line.

It was about 8.10 when the packed Poole train rounded a curve between steep embankments just before Clapham Junction. The driver had been given clearance by all the signals but ahead of him he saw the back of the Basingstoke train. He rammed on the brakes, but was too late to avoid a collision and the Poole train ploughed into the back of the stationary Basingstoke train. As it did so it tilted into the path of the Haslemere train on the adjoining line. Just as at Harrow, three trains had collided with tremendous force leaving victims mangled in the wreckage. Although the Haslemere train was empty, there were about 1,000 passengers on the other two. At Harrow it had been the passengers in the rear coaches of the local train who took the worst of it; at Clapham it was those in the front two coaches of the Poole train.

Ken Hines first saw the scene from the air. A call from the police on the emergency line at his surgery in South Woodford in east London had alerted him shortly after the crash. As a BASICS doctor, he had a direct line to the London Ambulance control, and called to check that he was needed. Dr Hines had a longstanding arrangement with the M11 traffic police for just such an emergency. They would collect him and his fellow BASICS doctors from a piece of waste ground at Chigwell which was near the police control layby. On the day of the Clapham disaster he was offered a helicopter. Two doctors from his BASICS team flew on ahead and the helicopter returned to pick him up.

When we got to Clapham the pilot asked me if I would like to take a look at the scene, and he circled it, which was very useful. You can take it all in, which you can't really do on the ground. We landed in a small park and then a police car took us to the crash site, which was an awkward one because there was a steep embankment. As I arrived steps were being cut into it to make it easier to get the injured out.

I went to the Ambulance Control Unit to report in and then looked for the medical incident officer and asked him what I should do. He wasn't sure, so I went down on to the track and met a lot of the ambulance people I know. We

decided to go the length of the trains to see what had still to be done. I moved along the train identifying quite a number of people who were dead. Most of the live casualties were being well attended to and moved away. I simply went on until I came to a problem which wasn't being resolved. My colleagues were doing the same thing from the other end of the train. Three of us ended up looking after one long-term entrapment each.

Dr Robin Winch, who had flown out in the helicopter before Ken Hines and was, like Ken, a veteran of the Moorgate disaster in 1975, took over as medical incident officer while Ken and the other two BASICS doctors got down to the business of trying to save the lives of the victims who were so tangled in the wreckage that it would take a long time for the fire brigade to free them.

One passenger who had been in the guard's van of the Basingstoke train was trapped when the Poole train rode over it. When Dr Hines got there three ambulancemen – not quite, at that time, fully fledged paramedics, but they had received advanced training – were keeping the man alive.

From the guard's van we could see his head and his arms, down about as far as his nipples, but the rest of him was lost in the tangle of metal. By going under the train you could see his legs, one of which was almost amputated, and he was losing a lot of blood. Because of the way he was trapped we couldn't stop the blood. What we had to do was to put fluids in his arm to make up for what he was losing through his leg.

By the time Ken Hines had got to Clapham there was, he says, an eerie silence, and a quiet camaraderie among the rescue workers. Earlier, when the ambulances first arrived, it had been different. Peter Ellison from Fulham Ambulance Station was one of the first on the scene, in spite of having been misdirected to Clapham Junction station at first. (The crash was actually on the lines approaching the station.)

One of the first sights I saw was a head hanging out of a window with the body inside. I had only qualified as an ambulanceman in June. My initial reaction was one of panic, but then I saw Barry [Barry Davies, an in-service training officer] and felt easier. I was with people. We set up drips. Everybody was shouting and there was mayhem for about twenty minutes.

As he moved through the wreckage, Peter came across the man trapped in the guard's van. 'He was screaming in pain. Barry and I were there first and then Martin arrived. Martin filled him with entonox, which seemed to pacify him. He was conscious. I had to go and get more gas so Martin took over.'

Entonox, an anaesthetic, pain-relieving gas, is often used at disasters as it acts quickly. Martin Flaherty, another Fulham Ambulance Station man, was what we would now call a highly trained paramedic. He had been

Ambulance crews had the medical skills to treat the injured in the wreckage of the Clapham crash and to save lives at the scene.

---

conducting a training course when he heard about the crash, and on the spur of the moment he took eighteen trainees with him. When he got there he asked if anyone was trapped and was directed to the man in the guard's van. By then, a doctor who had been a passenger on the train was with him. She left and Martin took over.

He was thrashing about and unmanageable; throwing himself around. I could tell from the way he was trapped he was not coming out for a long, long time. I knew he would need fluid to keep him alive and I knew I needed a doctor – I could not give him fluid forever. He would need pain relief and blood.

Even the most highly trained ambulance crews are not allowed to give or arrange blood transfusions, and there is a problem with these anyway because blood types need to be cross-matched. Two units of blood substitutes can be given by paramedics, but only a doctor can authorize more. In this case, the doctor who turned up to give medical guidance was Ken Hines.

Another ambulanceman with advanced training, Bob Dobson, had also found the man trapped in the guard's van, but from a different angle. Dobson crawled under the wreckage of the train and could see a man's legs. He did not know then that Martin Flaherty and a colleague were attending to the other end of the trapped man. Eventually Ken Hines relayed information between them, and went himself to look under the train. Dobson remembers:

I felt something dripping on my head and neck so I put my hand out and a lump of human fat and flesh fell into my hand. I just flung it away as fast as I could. I looked around and there was not a whole torso in sight. The space I was in was very small. I was cramped up for several hours. We were working to free the guy but his legs were badly trapped. The fire brigade were around and they were trying to work out a way of getting him out. They tried to lift the train off him and to put airbags in the carriage above me. I was worried for my own safety – I kept saying, 'Remember we are down here.'

It took three hours to free the victim. In the meantime, Ken Hines and the three ambulancemen watched his every move. They had a defibrillator and an up-to-the-minute portable monitor which tracked his heartbeat in case he had a heart attack. All the while the

In a skilled and delicate operation, a casualty has been freed from the wreckage by firefighters working alongside paramedics and doctors at Clapham.

rescue team were wondering whether they should knock him out cold, or amputate his leg to help free him. When the fire brigade finally cut and hauled their way through to release him, Dobson was underneath.

I had already given the man an anaesthetic to make him unconscious. At that point his legs had been pressed together, but now the pressure was gone and his main artery or something just burst and I was covered in blood. It was like a river and I had nowhere to go – it showered all over me. I shouted to the doc, 'You have to stop him bleeding,' and he took over and I pulled away.

This team of one BASICS doctor and three ambulancemen with advanced training saved the life of the victim. He lost a leg, but after treatment at St Stephen's Hospital, Fulham, he recovered. Dobson, who had spent so long tending the man from below, found himself in the ambulance taking him to hospital, but he did not recognize him because he had only seen his legs.

For the majority of the seriously injured who were not trapped in the wreckage or could be extricated quickly by the fire brigade, the trained ambulance crews were able to provide drips and other immediate care to stabilize their condition before they were taken to hospital. This advance – and the corresponding training, medical supplies and other equipment – is a massive change from the time of the Harrow crash. Another ambulance training officer who went to Clapham, called out on his day off, was John Pooley, whose father had been an ambulanceman at Harrow.

It would have been unbelievably different at Harrow. My father joined the ambulance service in 1938. He was given a hat, the ambulance to drive and told to get his first-aid certificate in the first year – but nobody checked. Many people had internal injuries at Clapham. What we were able to do for them, which no one could do at Harrow, was to give them fluids. We kept them alive while they

Although it happened close to a road, the site of the Clapham train crash and the close tangle of carriages made rescue work very difficult.

just think, 'This is serious: I am going to die.'

Barry Davies, another ambulance in-service training officer who was at Clapham, believes a big difference from Harrow was the fact that ambulance crews led the way and went into the wreckage to be with victims rather than waiting for them to be freed. Davies himself spent more than four hours with a man who was trapped by his ankles, hanging upside down.

We got talking, so I knew he was reasonable. I put up a line [drip] and put him on oxygen. At that stage the firefighters were starting to cut through the wreckage. There was so much rubbish falling down that I had to cover my bloke. It was very intense, just me and him in this tiny space. I kept reassuring him and tried to keep him talking. You talk about anything – personal things. Sometimes you end up repeating yourself and having the same conversation twice.

Because of a mix-up of telephone calls between the ambulance service and the hospitals, the medical teams set off late. The accident happened at around 8.10am, but the site team from St George's Hospital in Tooting did not leave until 8.56am. Although there were four doctors appointed as medical incident officers, none could be contacted immediately by the accident and emergency consultant, Lindsay Stevens, so she sent in an orthopaedic surgeon, Paul Calvert, who had no training for this essentially administrative work.

Calvert should have gone to a cupboard to pick up the special jacket which would have identified him as the incident officer but he rushed off without it. In theory the medical flying squad from the hospital should have set up the triage point, sorting victims according to the seriousness of their injuries. But this had already been done by the ambulance service – the first patients were arriving at St George's at 9am, only four minutes after the medical site team left for the scene of the accident. as Lindsay Stevens and her colleague Richard Partridge, then a senior registrar in Accident

were in the wreckage. If we had not been able to do that they would have bled to death. Also ambulance staff are trained to keep the airways free. A lot of this basic training would have helped save people in 1952. Then people would have just been scraping up the bodies and rushing them to hospital.

Now we treat at the scene of the accident. We stabilize and then get the victims to the hospital. If they are stable there is then no need to rush it. If a patient is in an ambulance doing 60mph with the lights flashing and siren sounding they and Emergency at St George's, wrote in *Injury* magazine in 1990: 'By the time the site medical officer was in position, the London Ambulance Service had effectively triaged most patients and the first wave of severely injured reached us at 9am. The site medical officer's role in triage then was limited.'

Back at the hospital, the Accident and Emergency Department had its own triage system, though it was at one point bypassed by the arrival of two minibuses of casualties brought by Emmanuel School and allowed in through a side entrance. The headmaster and pupils from the school, which is next to the scene of the accident, were the first people into the wreckage, a drama which greatly excited the popular press at the time. The schoolboy heroes included twelve-year-old Terry Stoppani, who was honoured with the *Daily Star* Gold Award for Bravery (along with just about everyone else at the scene) for helping the walking wounded out of a mass of severed limbs and torsos and leading them to the school, where a casualty station was set up. 'He saved fifty lives,' trumpeted the *Daily Star*, which is perhaps rather more than the entire army of emergency service personnel would claim for that incident.

This kind of tabloid hyperbole does nothing to raise the level of popular understanding of how disasters like Clapham are handled. The immediate task of saving lives usually falls to the first ambulancemen or women on the scene, who often have to take in a chaotic state of affairs very rapidly and to begin basic medical care before a doctor arrives. It is a very tough job, requiring iron self-discipline and a cool head. At Harrow the accounts of ambulancemen suggest that they just took whoever they found first to hospital and came back for more, regardless of the seriousness of injury. Today that would be regarded as incompetence.

The ambulance incident officer at Clapham was Hugh Chambers. He was on his way to work when he was alerted at 8.16am and was at the scene by 8.23. His first call when he saw the scale of the crash was: 'Make ambulances

twenty.' He recalls: 'Then it was a question of exploring the scene with the fire brigade and seeing what was what. You have to stand back at this point and not get drawn in, even if someone shouts, "Over here, over here!" The ability to stand back comes with training.' Confident that he could classify the injured from his advanced training, Chambers surveyed the scene, resisting the temptation to be sidetracked into rescuing individuals, so that he could assess the disaster as a whole and deploy his staff to best advantage. Nobody but the Americans did this at Harrow, where triage was non-existent.

Chambers set up a temporary casualty clearing station for those with minor injuries in a nearby pub and began to organize the parking of ambulances and loading of casualties. He then went into the wreckage with the fire brigade to get an idea of what the longer-term problems were going to be.

One of the most difficult things in a situation like Clapham is dealing with people who may be trapped and lying next to a dead body. You have to arrange a way of treating the live person without letting them know that the person close by is dead.

In the carriages there were people sitting on seats. Some were quiet, others were gazing ahead, totally stunned. People were saying, 'What is happening?' Others were just coming out of a faint. There were personal belongings and briefcases scattered everywhere. And among all the dust, smoke and smell of sulphur was a really strong smell of perfume – a bottle had been shattered in the crash.

When you come across someone you go back to basics. Are they breathing? Maintain airways. Then you think about giving fluids to reduce shock, and painkillers. Then you think about other things: let's face it, there is no point looking at someone and thinking, 'We will have to take his leg off,' unless you have checked his breathing.

At Harrow ambulancemen would not have known about crush syndrome, though doctors would have done. Everybody at a medical scene today would know that the liver and kidneys can be damaged if a part of the body is crushed. At Clapham we did save lives, and we relieved a lot of suffering. Modern medical care on site, better-equipped vehicles – these things all helped to save lives. Saving lives gives you a very warm feeling.

Back at St George's, and at another two hospitals which took a few patients each, casualties were being assessed and treated from 9am onwards. The brand-new Accident and Emergency Department at St George's Hospital, which had been opened only a week before the crash, was dealing with the injured at an impressive rate. By 10.10am they had taken in 119 casualties and had assessed and treated all of them by 11am. Of the patients who were taken to St George's, three died and another three were left 'mentally or physically disabled'. On the first day twenty-one operations were performed, five on the second day and seventeen subsequently.

At Clapham, as at all major disasters, notwithstanding the value of triage and 'stay and stabilize' methods, the aim is still to get casualties in need of life-saving surgery to hospital as quickly as possible. In that sense 'scoop and run' is still the policy. Attempts to introduce mobile surgical units were all abandoned long ago, and nobody argues for them any more. Even so, the contrast between the response of ambulance crews and doctors at Harrow and that at Clapham provides a clear illustration of the enormity of the changes that have come about in the intervening thirty-six years. Yet the medical arguments about the proper role of immediate care are still not resolved. How much should be done for casualties at the scene of an accident or disaster? Those who are sceptical about the use of paramedics and the role of BASICS doctors have mocked their efforts by saying they have turned the principle of 'stay

and stabilize' into 'stay and play', and indeed there is perhaps a danger of taking the concept too far. As the range of medical treatments paramedics are authorized to give is widened from the present narrow but critical procedures there is a risk that they might be so confident about their ability to save lives at the scene that they delay taking casualties to hospital too long.

Whether or not the special skills of the BASICS doctors were needed at Clapham has been disputed by doctors from St George's Hospital Accident and Emergency Department, who felt that there were too many doctors there. But Dr Ken Hines argues that their particular expertise, rather like that of the American medical teams who arrived at Harrow, was valuable. The crux of the matter is this: the conditions in which BASICS doctors and paramedics regularly work are a world away from those of an accident and emergency department in a hospital. Ken Hines and ambulanceman Bob Dobson are more familiar with the noise of the fire brigade's cutting equipment than with the calm intensity of the operating theatre. Their medical task may be limited, but it is vital. Ken Hines says:

It is team work, it has to be. We are familiar with what the fire brigades can do and we work with them. With the paramedics, who are superb technicians, I can make the best use of my medical skills. They need a doctor present for clinical decisions, to perform some advanced procedures such as chest drains, the administration of anaesthetic drugs, and to decide on volumes of fluids to give in drips. Our aim is to deliver the casualty to a hospital with his or her condition stable so that he is ready for the operating table.

Although BASICS has been a national organization of local schemes since 1977, and has a growing number of hospital doctors among its membership of 2,000, there are still those who regard them as 'enthusiastic amateurs'. One hospital consultant at Clapham, irritated rather than relieved by the arrival of Dr Hines, asked: 'If he is bored being a GP and wants to work in accident and emergency, why doesn't he get a job as a consultant?' Hines' response is firm.

When I was a junior hospital doctor I worked in the Accident and Emergency Department for over a year. I regularly rode on ambulances working with crews. In those days there were no careers as a consultant in accident and emergency work. Today things are different; there is now a career structure in emergency work. But I enjoy being a GP. I have continuity of care of patients and their families, not just care for a few hours in an accident department.

In the car park by his family practice in South Woodford is Dr Hines's white Volvo estate, its ambulance-style emergency lighting on the roof, the back packed with his BASICS equipment, which is similar to that carried by ambulances. Only very occasionally will his emergency phone call him out to anything more dramatic than a road accident, but with the M11 traffic police helicopter he and seven other doctors in the North-East Metropolitan Accident Unit can cover the whole of Greater London, the area inside the M25 motorway which encircles the capital. Since 1975 they have sent teams to the Moorgate tube crash of that year, to the King's Cross fire of November 1987 and to many other infamous incidents such as terrorist bombings and chemical explosions. They train regularly with the other emergency services in simulated exercises.

Over the years, the recognized founder of BASICS, Dr Ken Easton, has campaigned for the creation of accident and emergency departments in hospitals and for the abolition of the old Cinderella status of casualty departments. (Although it is still common to use the term 'casualty departments', strictly speaking, these have become accident and emergency units since the 1970s with recognized specialists. By contrast, the old casualty departments were staffed by consultants and junior doctors working shifts as extra chores.) Nearly all this work and organization has been achieved with the help only of charitable funds and one small grant from the Department of Social Security.

Almost all the newspaper reports on the Clapham crash ignored or were not aware of BASICS and took the advanced training of ambulance workers for granted. But the official inquiry report by Mr Justice Hidden QC did recognize BASICS, and gave the organization a pat on the back. It was a rare instance of official approbation for what is surely, despite the residual cynicism of some hospital doctors, one of the most remarkable movements in the history of postwar emergency services.

Everyone agrees that if Clapham happened again tomorrow, the emergency services would be even better organized, equipped and trained than they were in 1988. The 1980s gave the emergency services a great many disasters on which to test their state of readiness and the need for the kind of high-tech first aid now available is universally recognized. The 'therapeutic vacuum' highlighted by Professor Gogler in Germany back in the 1960s is being filled.

But from the outset those who began to tackle the problem of creating modern emergency services to deal with the spate of road accidents in the 1960s realized that this was not simply a matter of better training for doctors and ambulancemen and women. If the fire brigades of Britain had not become involved in rescue work, the efforts of doctors and paramedics at a disaster like Clapham would have been futile. At Harrow in 1952 firemen pulled at the mangled trains with their bare hands and attacked them with hacksaws. The only effective cutting gear was a hot oxyacetylene burner which would at best have scorched the trapped passengers. Worse was the constant danger that it would set fire to the broken timbers of the trains, and so it could only be used to free the dead. At Clapham the whirr and hammering of the firefighters' incredible extrication gear broke the eerie silence of the scene as the stupefied victims hung on to life and awaited their release.

Chapter Two
THE JAWS OF LIFE

Back in the 1950s, before the first motorway was opened and when teenagers dreamed of owning a car like the American kids they saw in films at the cinema, at the very birth of our modern car-owning democracy the most celebrated highway in Britain was the old A1 – or the Great North Road – which runs from Islington in north London to Edinburgh.

There were no sections of dual carriageway then, but the traffic was light, for to own a motor car was still something of a status symbol and the lorry drivers taking their loads of vegetables and building materials from town to town were still a bit like frontiersmen, and had a great camaraderie of the road.

To the modern motorist, angered by a plethora of cones on motorways and forced continuously to cut his or her speed from

A pile-up on one of Britain's old A roads in Kent, in 1960, when road accidents were rising fast.

35

A 1955 police accident map of Catterick,
Yorkshire, a blackspot on the Great North Road.

no hard shoulder, and no lights at night. The *Picture Post* reporter, Trevor Philpott, presented the catalogue of disaster on each stretch: seventy-four people had been killed on one twenty-four-mile section in Hertfordshire since 1951; on the two miles through Stevenage, ten people had been killed in the previous three years; and at Catterick Bridge in Yorkshire there had been fourteen crashes between March and November 1955.

One of the worst black spots was Catterick village itself, with twenty-nine accidents, one of them fatal, in a six-month period in 1955. It was here, as it turned out, that a few years later, with the carnage still growing, some pioneer attempts were made to equip the emergency services with the tools to rescue the victims of road accidents. In those days the police, fire and ambulancemen who went to the scene of an accident carried practically nothing to release and save the lives of those trapped at the steering wheel or in the crushed cab of a lorry. Many victims bled to death as a result. Often the fire brigade did not turn out at all if there was no danger of fire.

The fire brigade still has no statutory duty to attend a road accident or train crash, or to carry out a whole range of rescue work which today we have come to expect of them. Their job, officially, is to put out fires. Yet the demands put on what the fire brigade calls 'special services', which includes rescuing the victims of road accidents, has grown exponentially since the 1950s and nowadays all brigades have rescue tenders with an astonishing array of equipment, such as the cutting and spreading equipment from the

70mph to 50mph, conditions on the old A1 might sound quaint and idyllic, but they were far from that. In 1955, *Picture Post* magazine described it as 'the bloodiest country lane in Britain', under the headline 'THE GREAT NORTH ROAD: 400 MILES OF DEATH'. This 'ugliest and most terrifying country lane in the world' was a killer on a scale far greater than any motorway or A road today. There were only two lanes, one going north and one south,

USA known as 'the jaws of life'. All this has largely been acquired on a piecemeal basis and with little central government backing or extra financial support. The way in which the road accident rescue work of the fire brigade grew – through the efforts of individuals who were horrified by the scenes they witnessed at RTAs (road traffic accidents) and fought to find a way of saving more lives – is a classic case in the history of emergency services.

In the 1950s, thirty years before BASICS was formed, Dr Kenneth Easton was a family doctor in Catterick, where both his home and his surgery were within earshot of the Great North Road. On the other side of the road lived a local policeman. Both professionals were regularly called to road accidents nearby.

'The policeman and I used to leave the bedroom window open at night so we could hear the crashes, and we would just go off and find them,' says Dr Easton. 'My wife Janet always got up while I dressed, to get things ready.' Janet Easton recalls:

It was a race between the policeman and my husband to see who could get there first. I would go down in my dressing gown and open up the garage, get his doctor's coat ready, and put it on him. Later, when we had an emergency light, I would put that on top of the car: it fitted with a magnet. Then I would go back to bed, although I was often woken again when casualties came in.

Dr Easton and his wife might be woken up three nights a week. When the doctor and the policeman got to the scene of the accident there would not necessarily be a fire engine there, and even if one was called out the lack of extrication equipment meant its value was limited. Ron Atkinson, who joined the local fire brigade in

1949, recalls:

All we had were crowbars and hacksaws. It was terrible that we hadn't the equipment to get the poor sods out. I argued for having an emergency tender, but the chief officer said, 'Atkinson, these people who drive through don't pay rates.' I argued left, right and centre, but the chief did not want to know. In those days it was the undertakers who did the extrication, the firm of Wilson and Willoughby.

All along the A1 there were garages which sent out crane lorries to tow in broken down and damaged cars and goods vehicles, and it was sometimes left to these recovery trucks to extricate trapped people in crushed vehicles. Six miles from Catterick was the Londonderry Garage, next to a small hamlet right alongside the A1. Ron Exelby took over his father's haulage business there in 1947 when he came out of the RAF. So many ex-servicemen bought up ex-army vehicles and went into haulage that Ron got out of that trade and turned the Londonderry Garage into a service and recovery business. He bought a crane for towing cars off the road, and then a much

---

Yet another smash on what was known as 'Death Hill', Farningham, Kent, in 1968.

larger one which could handle the largest lorries on the A1. Almost straight away, in 1948, he found himself in the business of trying to save the lives of motorists.

Sometimes I was there before the police. I was well known by the truck drivers, and as I was so close to the A1, they would sometimes knock me up and say, 'There's an accident along the road, and it looks pretty bad,' and I would be off. I would start trying to rescue anyone who was trapped – you had to try to get them out or they would die. You would be there on your own. I suppose I saved lots of lives. I knew how trucks were made because I had a repair business, and that knowledge helped when it came to trying to get them apart.

Ron Exelby often heard a tap on his window from the local patrol and the call, 'Get yourself out, Exelby! He says: 'Even now if I am woken when I am asleep I am immediately 100 per cent awake after all those years of being called out and having to go straight away.'

The methods Ron used for extrication were by today's standards quite crude – chains attached to a cab to try to pull it away from a trapped driver; a simple hacksaw, jacks and other bits of garage equipment. But he was the only one who could do the job. 'You were on a wing and a prayer, and often you did not know if you had killed the person while trying to get them out.'

Ron was still turning out with his crane in the mid-1960s. He often arrived at the scene of an accident before the fire brigade and got to work as usual to free anyone trapped. He was sometimes appalled by what happened when the fire brigade turned up. This was thirty years ago, but to this day Ron is indignant. While some fire brigades were getting hand-pumped hydraulic cutters in the 1960s, others had only oxyacetylene burners to cut open cars and trucks. Just as at the Harrow train crash, these were entirely inappropriate when someone was trapped. Ron remembers:

On one occasion two gravel lorries had crashed into each other and one of the drivers was trapped. I arrived to see a fireman walking towards the man, lighting an oxyacetylene burner – I could see the blue flame. The driver had the steering wheel in his chest and couldn't move, and this fireman is coming towards him to cut off the steering-wheel column with equipment which would have burned the man's legs or set fire to him. There was a look of terror on his face. I grabbed the burner and shouted, 'Piss off!' I got a hacksaw from the other firemen and gave it to the driver to cut himself out. When he was free he said to me, 'I'm jolly glad you came.'

In the same period a lorry spun off the road right next to Ron's garage and ended up with its wheels in the air. The roof was compressed nearly down to the levels of the seats, crushing the driver in his cab. He was pinioned by the weight of the lorry and gasping for breath.

My jib wasn't big enough to reach the lorry so I got a hydraulic jack and with a piece of wood began to jack the lorry up. It was very tense, because the jack could easily have slipped in the mud, and the weight of the lorry springing back would have broken the man's neck. I was sweating as I jacked the cab up. Then a fire engine arrived and a fireman came running out and jumped on to the upturned lorry. I was swearing at them, shouting at them to get off. They were enthusiastic, but they had very little knowledge.

When the fire brigade began to get involved in this kind of rescue work, nobody approached Ron Exelby to ask him about his experience and the techniques he had learned from the years he had been releasing trapped motorists. 'There was no training then and they had to learn from experience, as I had, and I was upset they did not ask me what I knew. It was a backward step, really.'

It took a long time for firemen to learn how to safely extricate trapped motorists without injuring them or affecting their chances of survival. As always with the emergency services, all innovations appeared locally at first, and one fire brigade might at any one time be far ahead of another in its techniques and expertise. In the Sixties, however, nobody was very good at it.

George Walker, a lorry driver, was one of those who experienced the primitive rescue services on the A1. In October 1960, his lorry loaded up with pylon bars destined for the new Dungeness B Power Station, he was following a tarmac lorry with a trailer. The trailer, which had three men on it, broke loose. George slowed down to avoid them, while at the same time trying to keep his load on. It was chained, but he knew it would slide off if he stopped too suddenly. While he was braking one of the men jumped off the trailer and ran in front of him, forcing him to swerve. His cab went over the edge of an embankment, and the pylons shifted and trapped him in his cab with a badly gashed leg. One by one the police, the fire brigade and a doctor turned up. Some suggested cutting through the pylon bars, but George stopped them – he remained conscious throughout – because the whole load would then have shifted and pushed him down the bank. In effect, he controlled his own rescue.

'Get a lorry in the field across the road,' I told them, 'and get some chains around the pylon bars and hold them so they don't go down the bank side. Then get a chain on the trailer as tight as possible and get a lorry in behind me.' The traffic had all built up and a lorry had to come all the way round to the other side of the field to get in. They got the chains on and I said: 'When you're ready, give them a hard pull.' That's what they did,

Ron Exelby, who ran a vehicle recovery garage, extricated trapped victims from their cars in the years before the fire brigade became involved.

and I just fell straight through the floor. The police pulled me out from beneath the lorry. The ambulance stood by.

At the hospital George thought he had lost his leg, but they managed to pin it together. 'I was three years in the hospital, on my back all the time, and I had an operation nearly every week. It was terrible. I couldn't turn. I had a year of physiotherapy when I came out, so I was off work for four years.'

For risking his own life to avoid killing the man who jumped off the trailer, George was awarded a *Daily Herald* 'Workers' VC'. He eventually went back to truck driving. Had he not stopped the fire brigade from cutting the pylon bars with their oxyacetylene burner, he would almost certainly have been dead.

As the wrecked vehicles and the shattered bodies piled up on the A1 from the early 1960s, the sense of frustration among those so ill-equipped to help became acute. Nobody then had any statutory duty to improve the situation. At one point the local police at Northallerton tried to address the matter. Ted

Field, then head of the traffic unit, recalls:

> The authorities refused to help so we decided by devious means to get the cash together to buy some first-aid gear and a cutting saw, the sort you would use in building for cutting stone. We had no money for anything more sophisticated, but we had some gear before the fire brigade. On one occasion a Rover had hit a bridge and was crushed and we could not get the man out so Ron Exelby towed it to the aerodrome nearby and we cut him out there.

It was Dr Easton who finally made a decisive move towards rectifying the desperate state of affairs in Catterick. An accident in 1965 was the turning point:

A badly-injured lorry driver is stretchered away after a crash with a car in west London in 1961.

> I think it must have been early morning. A lorry had gone into the back of another one and the one at the rear had a badly smashed cab. The metal was all crushed and the driver was trapped, and his passenger's leg had been amputated. I had a desperately ill driver with chest and other injuries, and a passenger bleeding to death. The fire brigade did their best to pull the lorries apart with cables, but they kept breaking and catapulting back. There were vegetables on the lorries and they were falling all over us.

Ron Exelby was called out with his big crane, but he was six miles away and he could do only 24mph 'downhill with a fair breeze'. It took him an hour. By the time he got the trucks apart the passenger was dead, although miraculously, the driver survived. 'I felt sick and fed up,' Dr Easton says. 'I had constantly asked for things to be improved, but nothing was being done. It was the last straw.'

Dr Easton wrote to the Home Office and asked for the fire brigade to be given better equipment. He was told it was not the brigade's job to go to road accidents. He tried campaigning in Parliament and got nowhere. Eventually he called a meeting of police, fire brigades, ambulance services, local councillors, hospitals and an MP, and the county fire brigade was persuaded to get the equipment itself. The Road Accident After Care Scheme which Dr Easton founded in 1967 brought together all the emergency services and began to get them to work as a team at the scene of an accident, with the fire brigade taking on the role of extrication. This was a local project and the firemen still had little equipment and absolutely no training or experience. It was not until the end of the 1960s that training began for most brigades, and many years later still that real expertise was acquired.

Many hundreds, perhaps thousands, of accident victims who died in the 1960s could have been saved by modern techniques of extrication. It was always Dr Easton's argument that doctors, ambulancemen and firemen had to learn to work together. So the drive to improve the machinery and techniques of the fire brigade when they began to take on rescue work often came from those doctors who went out to accidents, mostly GPs like Dr Easton, or sometimes hospital doctors who realized that medical care was often needed during extrication. Without the doctor, the fire brigade's efforts might be futile, and without the firemen the doctor might be unable to administer treatment. They needed each other, and the support of the ambulance-men, who might arrive at the scene at the same time as the fire brigade.

Extrication techniques have evolved slowly over the years with the study of the nature of injuries and kinds of entrapment, and the acquisition, adaptation and invention of specialized machinery. Britain has not been especially inventive – much of the gear comes from abroad, where the release of road casualties inspired quite a few innovators. Typically, a fire brigade worked closely with a garage, or an individual fireman had an idea for what was needed and had the tool made. The oxyacetylene burner went out and in came metal saws, powered by air pressure, then mechanical cutters. Rescue tenders were built with compressors to drive the new machinery. The technology is now proudly displayed at trade exhibitions.

Although the fire service, which was nationalized in 1941–6, had no clear statutory obligation to provide rescue assistance on the roads, the Act of Parliament passed just after the Second World War which handed the fire brigades back to local authority control did

A victim of Britain's 'fastest ever crash' on the M1 in November 1959 – the Mercedes she was in was apparently travelling at 145mph.

allow them to get involved. Before the war, firemen had undertaken rescue work, saving the lives of animals that had fallen into ditches, retrieving stranded cats from the tops of trees and saving injured horses at a time when most traffic ran on a fuel of hay and oats. There were even special harnesses invented to lift horses clear of a wreck or a muddy hole. Yet at the dawn of the age of mass-motoring in the late 1930s, it seems the fire service was not acutely aware of the quite new responsibilities it was about to face as the only emergency service which could sensibly take on complicated road rescues. The problem had not yet really arisen as the bulky design of cars in those days meant that chassis were relatively robust and less likely than the more stylish designs of the 1950s and 1960s to crumple up in a crash.

When the war came, petrol rationing suppressed motoring, and the fire service in any case had much greater problems to cope with – tackling the blazes of the Blitz, for example. In his book *999: The Accident and Crash Rescue Work of the Fire Service,* Neil Wallington, a former chief fire officer, offers some statistics which show how small a part of the fire brigade's work road accidents used to represent. The pre-war London Fire Brigade, which covered the densely populated built-up area of the London County Council and was the busiest brigade in the country, answered sixty-one special service calls in the whole of 1927 and only 123 ten years later. In the 1950s a big city might answer 400 to 500 calls a year, smaller cities around 100.

Although London appears to have had the first purpose-built rescue tender as early as 1919, it was only in the Twenties and Thirties that these old open-topped engines became a familiar sight alongside the traditional fire pumps and turn-ladders. Before the Second World War there were 1,625 fire brigades in Britain, most of them clearly small and not especially well equipped. After denationalization in 1948 there were only 147, though many of these, as we saw in Chapter One, were combined with the ambulance service, and until the end of the 1950s firemen might be on

a fire engine one day and driving an ambulance the next.

With the change in car design in the 1950s and 1960s, and a steady rise in road traffic still using the old single-carriageway A roads which had no hard verges to save those who skidded or swerved to avoid an accident, the number of motorists who became trapped in wrecked vehicles grew steadily year by year. Garage owners like Ron Exelby developed a rough and ready expertise in extrication and many police forces, like the one serving Catterick, began to acquire their own tools for freeing victims. A few fire brigades began to re-equip newly commissioned rescue tenders, but this still formed a very small percentage of their work and there was no extra funding available for it. While the statistics on road deaths rose alarmingly, there was no national move to do anything about the grim toll of casualties except by those who felt they had a duty to deal with them, like Dr Easton and his wife who could hear what was going on through their bedroom window. There was much more general concern about the training and equipping of ambulancemen and ambulances than there was about the inadequacies of the rescue work of the fire service. Moves were set in motion to remove the ambulances from the jurisdiction of local authorities and attach them to the health authorities, a change which did not in the end happen until 1974.

But the fire service was coming under pressure to expand its responsibilities and expertise. The great catalyst which drew firemen into more and more rescue work at road accidents was the opening of the first motorways, from late 1959, and the first spectacular pile-ups which ensued. These were crashes on an unprecedented scale, akin to railway disasters, and often happened in fog when drivers failed to slow down to safe speed limits. It was not long before there was an outcry over 'motorway madness'.

Remarkably, nobody in authority appears to have given any thought to the new and especially difficult problem of going to the rescue on a motorway. As the late chief fire officer of Hertfordshire, Geoffrey Blackstone, commented: 'Hardly any existing fire stations and certainly none in Hertfordshire had been sited with 999 response to the new M1 motorway in mind.' There was none of the old camaraderie of the Great North Road on the motorways, which cut through open country, avoiding towns and cafés and the garages where men like Ron Exelby made a living retrieving crashed vehicles. And for the fire brigade and ambulances, getting on to motorways was difficult because there were relatively few access roads, and emergency vehicles could travel in only one direction.

It became obvious that one service had to take on the task of dealing with motorway pile-ups, and that it had to be the fire brigade. They had to instigate a new way of working, sealing off the danger from fast oncoming traffic by parking their emergency tenders and pumps – in case of fire – across the carriageway and providing firemen with luminous orange and yellow jerkins to make them easily visible by day and by night.

On the A roads, the old hands, the garage rescue men, were phased out as the fire brigade took on their work. But techniques and new equipment were slow to evolve. The newsreels of the day, which look comic now, were excited by the development of 'giant tin-openers', new kinds of jack, new air-powered saws, new chisels. There was always a worry with spilt petrol around that sparks flying from cutting gear or oxyacetylene burners would set the whole lot ablaze.

The new equipment was developed in a haphazard way. The firms that supplied the fire brigade with hydraulic power looked for tools that might be useful. This was how the Cengar saw came into being. Its name was a contraction of Central Garage, a firm founded in 1928 which was asked to adapt one of the hacksaws it made for industry to suit extrication. It was a great improvement on crowbars and handsaws, speeding up the rescue operation. Bedfordshire Fire Brigade pioneered a strong rubberized airbag which could be inflated by vehicle exhausts to provide a powerful lifting capacity.

By the mid-1970s some fire brigades had renamed themselves fire and rescue services for the first time, and the number of brigades was reduced from 147 to around sixty-six in 1974 as the smaller ones were closed down. It was still the case, however, that each brigade tackled the problem of road traffic accidents in its own way. All fire chiefs took a much closer interest in how extrication could be improved.

Getting a badly injured person out of the twisted wreckage of a car without harming him or her further is a task which requires a unique combination of skills. Before anything is done to free the victim immediate life-saving procedures must be carried out. Typically, people in the front of a car are trapped by their legs, and the driver is rammed into the steering wheel. The casualties will be losing blood and body fluids and struggling for breath. They are dying, and may even be technically dead, with no pulse, and yet, if tended to quickly enough, they can survive. Simply cutting someone out of a car could be a death sentence: many road-accident victims in the past have been killed by well-meaning passers-by who have dragged them from the wreckage, turning serious injury into fatal injury.

So before the cutting begins, whoever is first on the scene, in all probability a firefighter, has to make sure that the victim can breathe and will not bleed to death. When the cutting starts it must not be too rushed or too slow: the casualty needs to be extricated with the care an archaeologist takes in unearthing a precious piece of ancient porcelain. It has to be done little by little – no broken bones, no jolts, no fatal vibrations. Great care must be taken with spinal injuries if unnecessary disablement is to be avoided. Ideally, the firefighters themselves need to understand the physiology of the human body as well as the structure of the car. Medicine and mechanics go hand in hand, and knowledge of both is something to which those dedicated to the modern art of extrication aspire.

Although all fire brigades are much better

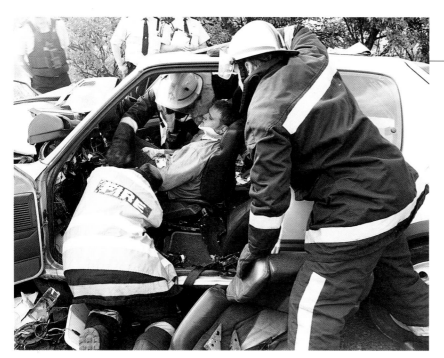

West Yorkshire firefighters perform the skilled mechanical surgery of extrication to free a motorist trapped in his car.

at extrication now than they were five, ten or fifteen years ago, some perfectionists in the service feel that in the light of modern knowledge about the medical care of road-accident victims and the quality of equipment, which is generally very high, the rescue work of firefighters still falls short of the best practice. Although the fire service training college situated at Moreton-in-Marsh in Gloucestershire offers world-renowned training courses in extrication, there are those who still see room for improvement.

Len Watson is one of those 'perfectionists'. Like Dr Easton, and others who have fought a lone battle for years to get things done, and gathered disciples around them, Len's vocation is to improve things. He joined the London Fire Brigade in 1968 to fight fires rather than dismantle vehicles, but like all firemen of that time he was soon on the road with the emergency tender to assist at road crashes. He had learned a bit of first aid, but had had no training in extrication – there was none in those days.

One of the first bad accidents I attended was in 1969. It involved a Rover and a Capri. There were five people in the Capri and one in the Rover, and they were all seriously injured. The guy in the Rover 90's knees were pinned and the two men in the front of the Capri, a heavy, classical car, were really badly trapped. The people in the back were also stuck because this was a two-door saloon. To contend with this, we were trying to prise open the doors of the Capri with crowbars and a pickaxe. After about an hour we got one door off. It was much tougher than we were. In the meantime, through breaking the windows, they managed to get the three passengers in the back out, but obviously, as I know now, this was at their expense, because this was no way to handle casualties at an accident of this magnitude [because of the risk of further injury].

And that commitment [the term firefighters use for this kind of rescue work], went on until maybe the three-hour mark. It was a very troublesome affair, and after all that time, all we'd done in terms of extrication was to remove a door and put in jacks and an alligator spreader to relieve the pinning on the feet and legs. Those two casualties in the front of the Capri died while we watched them. They died on us, and the only immediate care they got was from an ambulance person with very little training.

What's remarkable is that when we got back to the station we all felt good about it: that was a hell of a good job because it took us three hours. There were many accidents like that.

Len had joined the fire brigade at a time when tools like the Cengar saw and the zip-gun for cutting panelwork were becoming standard gear rather than special issue. 'They were brought into the station on a frame with cylinders, a pneumatic hacksaw and pneumatic chisel, and laid in the store until the following January, when the equipment was put on the truck. And that was it – we turned up at accidents and were supposed to use this stuff, but we still had no training.' The first time Len tried the Cengar saw was in an attempt to release a man trapped in his car upside-down after it skidded off a roundabout and buried itself in the wall of a garage.

It was very confined and we had a lot of trouble releasing him because we had not got the knack of this. We thought these tools were designed for the fire service – we didn't realize they came from the garage trade and had been adapted. But, bit by bit, we got him out and the man survived, to my surprise. Being able to open the door and cut it

away was easier than in the past, when you had to remove the pins holding the wreckage together, one by one, listening to all the screams and groans.

Len, like some other firemen, became frustrated with the lack of specialized equipment which he felt they needed and he knew existed in other brigades.

We kept asking for it and we were told that bad workmen blame their tools. We didn't really have any to blame. At some point we were introduced to a new cutter and a power spreader which was operated by a hand pump. The first time we took them to an accident – a pretty horrific smash – within thirty minutes we had actually taken the roof off the car, and the side door, relocated the steering

A pile-up on the M62 in Yorkshire. The need for new methods of road accident rescue resulted in the fire service's involvement in extrication.

wheel and released the pinning to the feet. It was controversial at the time: when we got back to the station we were asked for a debrief because we had done so much damage to the car. They said it was totally unnecessary. But for me the future of rescue was born on that particular night.

From long and, for Len, bitter experience, which went back to the days of adapted garage tools, he learned that it was possible to save many more lives with better techniques and equipment. He had known at first hand the frustration of doctors and ambulance crews as they waited while an extrication team from the fire brigade took up to two hours to lever and hack a victim free. The doctor who founded the London branch of BASICS, Robin Winch, regularly arrived at the scene of an entrapment. He taught Len something of the medical side of extrication. Dr Winch was later to write the foreword to Len's great labour of love, which bore the technically undramatic title *RTA, Persons Trapped, Vehicle Accident Rescue*, a weighty training manual. He published this at his own expense, with some sponsorship from the Dutch company HOLMATRO, which makes much of the most up-to-date extrication gear now in use.

Until 1984, Len Watson was a firefighter with a special interest in extrication. But it did not become his life's work until, in that year, he and another fireman were disciplined for disobeying orders at a ship fire and going to the rescue of a colleague. Banned from firefighting but still in the brigade, he put his energies into the study of extrication, in which he remained involved as part of his job until recently when he moved to London's Southwark Training Centre as an instructor. He began researching the subject and became obsessed with it. In 1989 he founded the Car User's Road Accident Extrication Society to promote good practice, and it organizes extrication competitions at national and international levels. Teams are given a task rather like those seen at the Royal Tournament, where artillery men put guns together against the clock. For the extrication championships a highly sophisticated dummy has been constructed which can be programmed to mimic accurately a range of crash victim injuries. With points deducted for errors and loss of time, the teams go in and demonstrate their skills at saving life.

Out on the road it is different. Len Watson feels that while equipment now is state-of-the-art, training and knowledge, which can only be acquired through experience, remains poor in many brigades. At the Southwark training centre of the London Fire Brigade, Len holds courses and seminars which bring together firefighters who will be working on extrication, ambulance workers and doctors. He also works with HEMS – the Helicopter Emergency Medical Service – based at the Royal London Hospital, which in daylight can get rescue teams out to a crash within five minutes.

Firefighters now are taught medical skills. They need them if, as is usually the case, they get to an accident before paramedics or doctors. But, as a result of his research, Watson believes most brigades put only about 10 per cent of their budget into RTA extrication, even though it plays a greater role in saving lives than the classic fire rescue. To a large extent this is because the fire service is still funded solely on the basis of its firefighting work and has to 'steal' from that budget to pay for new equipment and training for extrication. In fact, some fire brigades have recently threatened to withdraw from road-accident work because it has become too costly. Watson thinks insurance companies ought to make a significant contribution, as they do in some other countries.

But the situation has improved dramatically since Len Watson first set out with crowbar and pickaxe to dismantle a Rover and a Capri.

In those days I believe we saved about one life in four; now it is three out of four. Accidents are pretty horrific things. They stick in your mind just like seeing a human body in a fire does. The mutilation crashes can cause to the human body is mind-blowing. Extrication became a vocation for me because I wanted to do something to redirect all those wrong things I had done in the past.

Since the dark days of the 1960s, the death toll on the roads has fallen. Despite the vast increase in traffic there are fewer fatalities. Although motorways are the scene of spectacular pile-ups, they are generally safer than the old roads. The law making the use of seat belts compulsory must have saved many lives, and where immediate care from doctors and ambulance workers is well organized the chances of surviving are high, even for the most seriously injured.

The vast strides made in the fire brigade's equipment and technique must be another critical factor in the greatly improved survival rate. Nationally, Watson estimates, firefighters now operate the rescue tenders to deal with about 8,500 entrapments a year. Whereas back at the beginning of the 1960s, lorry driver George Walker had to direct his own rescue and spent three years in hospital and another year convalescing, it is likely that today he would have been released in less than an hour. The average time it takes for extrication, according to a recent study of London cases by the HEMS project, is forty-four minutes.

When he was involved in a pile-up on the M62 in Yorkshire just before Christmas in 1992, lorry driver Adrian Hussey was not freed quite that quickly, but he has an abiding admiration for the West Yorkshire firefighters who came to his rescue. He remembers it with a clarity born of the intense drama of his release. Adrian was the victim of a classic motorway smash. 'One minute I was driving along in fairly bright and sunny conditions – I was even wearing my sunglasses – and the next, just out of nowhere, I saw this bank of fog and vehicles over all four lanes.' He ended up in a pile-up, trapped in the cab of his lorry.

It seemed like an eternity, though it was probably only minutes, before the police arrived. They told me that the fire brigade were on their way and that they'd soon get me out. Then I remember a doctor trying to examine me. I was given some painkillers but they didn't do much good. I was still in terrible and constant pain.

About half a dozen firemen then arrived with all their cutting gear. In a way, they were just like nurses: they were incredibly kind and reassured me that they'd soon get me out and I'd be all right. They had these big metal cutters which I think they call the 'jaws of life'. First of all they got the hinges off the door so that they could then start working on the metal crushing me in the cab. Then they cut the steering wheel away, but when that didn't relieve any pressure on my stomach, they had to sever the whole steering-column shaft. It was such a relief when they eventually did that – I must have dropped about two inches, and although I was still in terrible pain, I was certainly more comfortable. Altogether it took about ninety minutes for them to release me.

They told me what was happening at every stage and they were real professionals who really knew what they were doing. When they finally lifted me out, I was absolutely elated. You could tell the firemen were relieved, too. I can see one fireman's face even now – he looked really satisfied and pleased with himself. I think firemen are fantastic people.

I know it sounds a bit over the top, but I am so grateful for what they did for me. I now worship the ground they walk on. If they didn't have such skills, I don't think I'd be here to tell the story.

Adrian is now back on the road after hospital treatment. 'There isn't a day goes by when I don't think about what happened. Every week I drive past the spot where I had the accident, so I'll never be able to forget it.'

The art of extrication, now a skill unique to the fire service, is the single most significant advance in life-saving in the postwar development of the brigade. Firefighters have taken on many other tasks in addition to their traditional role of putting out fires – the modern industrial world needs chemical plants, high-rise buildings with lift shafts in which people get stuck, motorways and millions of road vehicles which, with depressing frequency, smash into each other – but it is the road accidents that have provided the spur and the grim training ground for improvements. The skills acquired by all the emergency services from the routine work of rescue on the road can be applied to a considerable degree at less frequent, but more spectacular disasters such as train and plane crashes.

At the Clapham train crash in 1988, the firemen working alongside paramedics and BASICS doctors were able to use techniques of extrication developed on the roads. Although the structure of a train is obviously different from that of a car, and the cutting gear needs to be much tougher, many of the procedures detailed in the official Manual of Firemanship

are the same. The danger of fire, ever present at road accidents and plane crashes, which can be a serious danger to rescue workers as well as survivors, is less of a threat at a modern train crash, where the power is likely to be electric. But the fire service will be there, essentially in its acknowledged role as Britain's premier rescue service.

The huge range of necessary skills which have earned the fire brigade this accolade is reflected in the courses run at the Fire Service College at Moreton-in-Marsh in the Cotswolds. First set up in the mid-1950s on the site of a former RAF aerodrome as the Fire Service Technical College, it absorbed the former Fire Service College in Dorking in 1980. At Moreton, officers of all ranks are kept up to date on their skills and relay what they have learned

An impressive array of rescue equipment displayed by a Hampshire fire crew. From the late 1970s, nearly all fire brigades bought powerful cutting and spreading equipment form the USA and the Netherlands for extricating road accident casualties.

to their own brigades. Alongside the firefighting training areas, a section of motorway has been reproduced for rehearsing the techniques of handling pile-ups and toxic chemical spills. There is also a section of railway on which the methods of rescuing people from smashes like that at Clapham can be practised. The exercises are very realistic, and Moreton's specialist courses have an international reputation.

Yet there has been consistent reluctance on the part of successive governments to officially recognize the importance of the fire brigade's special-services work. In 1965 the Home Office told Dr Easton that fire brigades were not supposed to rescue people trapped in road accidents. Twenty years later, the view expressed in an official report had scarcely changed. 'Fire brigade resources are based on the need to provide adequate fire cover. Special-service work has to be undertaken within the resources provided for firefighting purposes.'

This attitude has ramifications for both routine road-rescue work and the role of the fire service at major accidents, train crashes and air disasters. Because the authorities refuse to regard the brigade, in terms of funding, at least, as anything more than a firefighting service, it is only in dealing with disasters which are clearly and primarily fires that the senior officer at the scene has a statutory duty to take charge of the whole operation. When there is a pile-up on the M1 or the M62, which emergency service should take control: the police or the fire brigade? This question has remained a running sore over the years, for in the confusion of the immediate aftermath of a disaster in which fire, or the threat of it, is only one of many problems, the answer is not clear. This is not to

West Yorkshire's rescuers in action, freeing a lorry driver trapped in his cab. Firefighters now save many more lives rescuing the victims of road accidents than they do getting people out of fires.

say that, between them, the emergency services are incapable of coming to an agreement about who does what in the event of what they prosaically call a 'major incident'. But controlling the chaos of a disaster as quickly as possible so that the work of rescuing people is not hampered by sightseers and confusion, ensuring that ambulances can get in and out and that the armies of the press and television are kept at bay, is just as crucial to the success of the operation as the medical and extrication skills of doctors, ambulance workers and firefighters.

The scene at the Harrow and Wealdstone crash described in Chapter One represents a stage in the solution of postwar disaster management which might be described as rock bottom. It has taken many years, and some shocking disasters, to improve the response and test the co-operative skills of the emergency services.

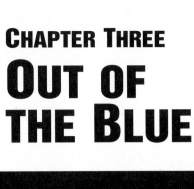

CHAPTER THREE
OUT OF THE BLUE

On an overcast and drizzly Sunday afternoon, Trevor Burke and his brother Paul were out walking the family dog near their home in Staines, Middlesex. They lived close to Heathrow Airport and were quite accustomed to the roar of jets lifting off and taking to the air a few hundred feet above their heads, banking into a flightpath to Europe. There was the drone of traffic, too, from the busy Staines bypass, where families returning from Sunday outings were driving nose to tail.

That particular Sunday was a long time ago, 18 June 1972, but Trevor Burke still recalls vividly the almost unbelievable experience he had when, at the age of thirteen, he was a witness to what was then the worst disaster in British aviation history. 'We heard an engine spluttering and stalling above the clouds,' he recalls. 'Suddenly, we saw this aircraft fall out of the sky – and it appeared to be coming

The grim expressions of firemen, ambulancemen, police and members of the public tell the tragic story of the Trident crash at Staines in 1972.

Because it was so quiet, with no fire or smoke, many rescuers thought when they first saw the wreck of the Trident Papa India that it was just another training exercise nobody had told them about.

straight for us. It fell like a stone. The impact was unbelievable, terrifying. It came down about a hundred yards away from us on the other side of a fence. Bits of debris fell beside us and there was a smell of kerosene.'

Trevor and his brother ran the half-mile to their home and fetched one of their neighbours, who was a nurse. 'We ran back to the plane. She started dragging bodies out and I heard a baby crying. There were four or five bodies strewn about and I nearly tripped over one. Then other people came from the bypass and started pulling people out – everyone thought the plane would go up in flames.'

Later Trevor learned that what he had seen was the end of a British European Airways flight from Heathrow to Brussels with 118 passengers and crew on board. The flight had been delayed and then, less than two minutes after take-off, as the Trident plane broke through the cloud it had stalled and plummeted to earth, the nose hitting the ground first and the tail breaking off on impact. The time was 5.11pm.

Because the plane had crashed so close to Heathrow a rescue operation should have swung into action according to plans laid down and rehearsed by the British Airports Authority. The sudden disappearance should have been noticed by Air Traffic Control, but it wasn't and so no immediate alarm was raised. In fact, news of the crash reached the emergency services in a series of ambiguous messages and it was a while before the scale of the disaster was understood. By that time, members of the public were at the scene, stunned by the horror of it and able to do no more than comfort the dying. Amazingly, several passengers, including a young girl, were not killed instantly by the tremendous impact which tore the interior of the plane to pieces and smashed much of its human cargo into a hideous mangled heap.

The Staines disaster is remembered now not only for the terrible scale of the carnage – all 118 people on board were killed – but for the remarkable scenes which followed. The wreckage, being so close to the busy bypass, drew huge crowds of sightseers, who were condemned in the daily newspapers as 'ghouls'. Macabre interest reached such a peak that roads became blocked and ambulances had difficulty getting to the scene. Officially, the British Airports Authority declared the Staines rescue operation a 'textbook affair', and much was made of the claim that the emergency services were at the scene within fifteen minutes.

It is impossible to say in retrospect whether there was any chance that those who were still alive after the plane hit the ground could have been saved. Certainly the coroner pronounced at the inquest that nobody could have survived the tremendous force of the crash. One passenger, a man, did live for three hours afterwards, long enough to be taken to Ashford Hospital, where he died. Some other survivors spoke a few dying words to those who tried to comfort them but expired before any ambulances arrived. Exactly how many people were still alive after the impact has never been established, and the question has long been considered irrelevant, for there was little chance that a swifter and better-organized rescue operation would have made a critical difference to the death toll.

Nevertheless, there were lessons to be learned from Staines, and there are those who went to the rescue who still ask themselves whether, had the impact not been so devastating, the crowds of sightseers, souvenir hunters and – so it was said – looters who jammed the roads around the site might have made it difficult or impossible to save lives. Obviously, communication between the services was very poor at Staines, and although the need to cordon off the area and keep a route clear for fire engines and ambulances was recognized, this was not achieved in time. The location of the crash made this especially difficult, but might a more co-ordinated effort between the services have kept the 'ghouls' at bay?

In the history of the emergency services and of the way they plan for and react to disasters of this kind, this has always been a critical issue. All such catastrophes begin as scenes of chaos. In this sense, Staines was 'textbook'. In the first hour or so after the crash there was an immediate response from bystanders, as well as from the first rescue workers on the scene, priests, photographers and others milling around in an unco-ordinated way desperately searching for survivors. By the time the

The Staines disaster is remembered by the emergency services for the terrible traffic jams that blocked roads to the site.

emergency plan could be put into action, the attempted rescue was well underway. This is not to say that between the time of, say, the Harrow crash in 1952 and Staines in 1972, no advances were made in disaster planning. But the unfolding of a rescue operation nearly always begins, as it did at Staines, with a rush of adrenaline as the first rescuers to arrive try to save as many lives as possible.

The need to seal off the site and keep roads clear is always one of the biggest problems whenever a disaster occurs. However well organized the emergency services are, others will inevitably reach the scene before them and they can only strive to control the confusion as quickly as possible.

At Staines nobody kept an exact log of who arrived at the wreckage at what time, but it is possible to gain some idea of what happened immediately after Trevor Burke and his brother ran home for help. Colin Sleep lived next door to the Burkes. He was a bus driver and a member of the St John Ambulance Brigade.

I heard a tremendous thump like a door slam. Then Trevor and Paul came, screaming their heads off. 'Plane crash,' they said. I was expecting a biplane. I ran with Mrs Castledine [the nurse] and pushed the fence down and there was this big Trident, it was unbelievable. There were passengers hanging out of the windows – we couldn't reach them – and bodies all over the place. Mrs Castledine went looking for survivors. She found one and we laid him out on a piece of fuselage, but his body was like jelly: all the bones had broken into little bits. We moved him away from the plane because we thought it was going to blow up.

Mrs Castledine talked to him and I picked up a coloured baby of about three years old. She was dead. I covered her with a bit of fuselage. Some time later we found her twin sister and we laid them on the ground together. In the plane all the seats had been pushed forward so that people's faces had hit the back of the seat in front of them. People had lost much of

their clothing, and their naked bodies were showing through the bases of the seats that had been pushed forward. There was little blood around, which meant instant death – aortas gone because of the terrific G-forces. Their hearts weren't pumping.

At this point there were still no police, ambulance crews or firemen at the scene. A priest arrived, then a *Daily Telegraph* photographer, Srdja Djukanovic. He had been taking pictures of the royal family in Windsor Great Park, but the weather was so bad that it was abandoned and he had headed back to London early. He was on the Staines bypass shortly after the crash.

Motorists were jumping out of their cars and I saw the tail of an aeroplane behind the trees. I rushed to it with my three cameras and there were already three people there. We looked for signs of life and shouted, 'Anybody alive?' But there was no answer. A priest knelt beside a dying man who had been dragged from the plane. I was in a daze and I couldn't take any photographs at first, but then I shot three rolls without knowing what I was doing. I had seen thousands killed in the war in Yugoslavia, and many other disasters, but this was not like anything I had ever seen before.

Meanwhile, the watch at Staines Fire Station were having a quiet afternoon in front of the television. John Shawyer, then a twenty-year-old leading fireman, remembers that they heard what they thought was an explosion which rattled the fire station windows. They went outside to look around, imagining that a boiler had blown up, or perhaps one of the oil storage tanks near Staines, but they could not see anything. They went back to the television and waited for the phone to ring, but no call came. Then a private car pulled up in front of the fire station and a man came up the driveway. Shawyer went out to meet him. 'Plane crash,' the man said. 'Staines bypass near the Crooked Billet.' Shawyer recalls: 'We hit the firebells and went and booked the incident on the wireless – "Priority," we told the girl back at Brigade Control. We got to the bypass and could tell where the plane was because there was already a Berkshire ambulance there and lots of private cars had stopped, too.'

Around the time the motorist alerted Staines Fire Station, Terry Henwood from Feltham Police Station took a call on the radio in his Panda car. It came from the Scotland Yard Information Room and said simply that there had been a report of a plane down near Staines bypass. Henwood remembers:

The impression they gave me was that it was something like a model plane; no big deal, they said. Apparently, Staines Police Station did not know about it. I drove for seven or eight miles and drew up where I thought it would be. I went down a bank into a field and then I saw the plane. My first impression was that everybody had got out – it was absolutely quiet, utter silence.

Henwood was the first policeman, and the first emergency service official, to arrive. His first instinct was to look for survivors. He went into the wreckage and called out: 'Is anybody there?' He heard a moan, a woman's voice.

The back part of the fuselage appeared to be empty and all the luggage had come down. I started walking over the luggage and then realized I was walking on dead bodies too. I got to where the stewardesses sit on their jump seats, and there was one still sitting there, strapped to her seat. One of her legs had opened out right down to her ankle, but there was no blood. It was extraordinary, I couldn't understand it. It still amazes me. I got a coloured guy out and dragged him on to the grass. He said 'My legs are hurting,' and I said, 'Don't worry, you'll be all right.' But he died within seconds.

While PC Henwood was in the wreckage, a second wave of police arrived, including Albert Wright and five or six other officers from Staines Police Station. Wright, now retired from the force, recalls:

This picture was taken just minutes after the Trident came down. The little girl, tended by a local woman and a priest, only lived for a few minutes.

We'd been told on the police radio that an aircraft had crashed. We raced out there not knowing what we were going to, although we had an idea that a light aircraft had gone down. On the bypass we saw a Panda car parked [Henwood's] and we looked over the fence and saw an aircraft in three pieces.

There was silence, and I thought, somebody's done a mock-up, this is an exercise we have not been told about. It wasn't until we got nearer that we saw a few dead bodies and a few police went to the aircraft, feeling pulses for signs of life. We started pulling bodies from the fuselage and forming lines to take out the luggage. We lined up bodies in rows of ten so that we could count them more easily.

Nobody, it seems, in these first frantic minutes, had tried to cordon off the site or to control the traffic that was building up. Even so, John Shawyer and his crew from Staines Fire Station got through to the bypass quickly enough. Shawyer says:

With another fireman we jumped over the fence. We didn't carry any hoses, just a fire extinguisher. Meanwhile, the other guys ran out the hose, but it was strange, because there was no smoke from the plane, and I couldn't believe it hadn't caught fire. There was a policeman there and I asked him, 'Have you made this a major incident?' But he was still trying to get through to someone on his radio, so I told the lads we had a major incident and to send a message back. Then we got stuck in, putting quarter-mile hoses to the main fuselage – there was a stench of fuel, and you could see a fuel haze shimmering feet above the grass.

The back section of the plane was flattened, so we could not get in, but I got on the starboard wing and started cutting my way in with a compressed-air hacksaw. I went in with Alf, another fireman, looking for survivors. We called out, but we didn't find any. Another fireman, Ted Frewin, got a survivor out and we were elated. Then we realized we weren't going to get anyone else, and we got depressed.

After being alerted by the motorist, Staines Fire Station had called Egham Station with the message that a plane had crashed 'somewhere between Egham and Staines'. Dave Fielding, now a senior officer for Surrey Fire Brigade, was then stationed at Egham. His pump set off to find the crash site, and on their way they met a police car and an ambulance. They all drove around looking for signs of the incident, but for a while they were lost. 'It was like the blind leading the blind,' Fielding recalls.

They drove on to the Staines bypass and saw the first fire engine parked there. Some motorists who had stopped told them where the crash was. Like PC Wright, Fielding could not believe at first that he was looking at a real disaster.

I went through a break in the hedge and there it was, just sitting there – no smoke, no fire – and my initial reaction was: 'This is pretty good, a very well-done exercise.' Then, as I approached the plane, I realized it wasn't an exercise. I saw a young Indian girl, dead, and there was a coloured guy hanging out of the broken fuselage with blood dripping from his tie. You have an idea of what a plane crash would be like – flames, fire, wreckage, lots of noise – but this wasn't like that at all.

Fielding met a nurse who told him there were survivors, so he went into the wreckage. The back part seemed empty, for all the seats had been torn away, but the front part was jammed with a wall of people and seats 8ft to 10ft high. 'It was as if a great ram had pushed everybody forwards,' he remembers. 'I climbed on to the wing and cut through with an axe, then I dropped inside and landed on a pile of bodies, feeling pulses to check if anybody was alive. Everyone I touched I thought was alive, and then I realized that I was feeling my own pulse, it was beating so hard with all the adrenaline.'

In these early stages of the rescue operation, perhaps the first fifteen or twenty minutes, there appears to have been no co-ordination. As they arrived bit by bit at the site, the emergency services overcame their initial disbelief that a jet airliner had fallen clean out of the sky and began to search for survivors. Radio communications were, by all accounts, useless, as each service had its own frequency.

Mick Hopper, who was the Surrey ambulance duty controller at their Banstead headquarters that day, says: 'We got no call from the police, no call from the airport: in fact, the only notification we ever had about the incident was a phone call from a member of the public. Communications were terrible in those days, because we had no means of keeping in touch with other emergency-service vehicles.' In 1972, the radio systems used were much less sophisticated than those today, but even now technology has not completely solved the problem. The pressure of calls in the wake of a disaster nearly always overloads systems which work well for routine emergency calls. However, co-ordination between services should, in theory at least, be much better now.

PC Albert Wright remembers that he began to be aware of the build-up of traffic on the Staines bypass. Ambulances were arriving, but there was a ditch between the bypass and the crash site which they had difficulty crossing. Finally they found a way into the field from the other side, through a narrow lane off Staines High Street.

When he looked over to the bypass, Wright could see a 'sea of non-moving vehicles'. He realized that they were surrounded not by people helping with the rescue operation, but sightseers.

The bypass had been totally blocked. It was then that I saw the thousands of people that had descended on the scene. They had gathered on the bank of the reservoir on the other side of the bypass, as if they were on the terraces at a football match. It was a good vantage point. It was incredible to watch them arriving like football crowds ten minutes before kick-off.

Down in the field there were people with young children on their shoulders. It was a bit ghoulish, but I suppose it is a natural thing to be inquisitive.

Neighbours of the Burke brothers also remember the build-up of the crowds. Terry Lyden had gone with the boys to the wrecked Trident and seen the devastation for himself, including a crew member, with blood trickling from his mouth, 'just about alive'. They went into the aircraft and it was fairly obvious that there was little they could do. 'By that time the rescue services had started arriving, and they said, "Thanks, go away,"' he says. 'I went back home. But the moment it came on the news, the crowds started in earnest. They were rushing through our gardens and I was trying to fend them off.'

The first news bulletins were broadcast on BBC Radio as newsflashes at 6pm, nearly forty minutes after the accident. As Terry Lyden says, it was after that that crowds swelled and hindered the ambulances and fire engines. But even before that, the bad traffic on the bypass and the location of the crash made the scene tricky to reach.

It was the build-up of the traffic jams for miles around that alerted Keith Atwill to the tragedy. Atwill and his wife were in their Salvation Army uniforms ready to attend their regular 6pm church service in Staines when they heard what had happened.

We ran over to the site carrying a tea urn, kettles and trestle tables. The fire, police and ambulance teams were already there, and there was a feverish activity around the cockpit area. Occasionally they would ask for total silence, listening for signs of life. We mucked in and started making cups of tea.

There were also many people not involved, just sightseeing. Some were on the bank of the reservoir, others in the field itself – thirty or forty people, some venturing within 15ft of the aircraft. One man had a five-year-old boy on his shoulders, and I thought, what's he doing here with a five-year-old? One police sergeant got so annoyed that he showed a body to them and they ran away. Later people came looking for things – not just souvenirs, wallets and things.

The traffic jams were terrible. I remember hearing one ambulanceman saying: 'We won't be able to get away with all this traffic. If anyone had been alive we would not have been able to get them to hospital.'

Policeman Albert Wright believes in retrospect: 'In the harsh light of day, we really should have got the traffic moving. We all rush to go to the scene, but there may be more important things to do. If we had had survivors, then people would have been dying in traffic jams, and that would have been bad.'

The rush of adrenaline which drives rescue workers first on the scene to save lives is a common feature of the accounts they give of their initial reactions to a disaster. It takes iron self-control to stand back and organize and leave the rescue work to others. It is for this reason that since the late 1950s there has been a principle that certain police officers, firefighters, ambulance workers and doctors are clearly designated as officers in charge to co-ordinate the rescue efforts of others. The value of this role was proved at Staines by its absence, and has been proved again many times since. It is not, of course, always easy or possible to put theory into practice. If, as is often the case, the rescue work is already underway when these incident officers arrive, by the time they begin to create order out of the chaos a critical phase in any disaster plan is over. At Staines David Sadler, who later retired from the Metropolitan Police as a commander, was the officer in charge.

I was telephoned at home and didn't get to the scene until about forty-five minutes after the crash. I picked up a police car at Hounslow, which helped us get through the traffic. I had left home in such a hurry that I had forgotten to put on my uniform. All I had was a trilby hat a and white coat somebody lent me, which I wore so that people could identify me.

I made up teams to secure the site, got my men to help carry away victims and organized property-recovery teams. Some army personnel were passing and I put them inside the cordons and got them to help with body evacuation.

There was a problem with vehicles on the bypass and I got my men to clear them away to allow the emergency vehicles to get in and out. Some of the public moved their cars when asked, but many had been abandoned so we had to clear them ourselves.

Sadler says that press photographers were a greater problem than the so-called ghouls, and some had to be evicted. As for the idea that this was a 'textbook operation', neither he nor any of the other rescue workers at Staines would agree.

We had the Heathrow Airport plan, of course, and could use that, for example with the handling of the bodies. But we didn't have the sort of formal plans there are today: they were more implicit than explicit, because each of the services knew their general role, which was simply an extension of what they did on a day-to-day basis.

I think we had been lulled into a false sense of security by a lack of disasters. The Trident crash woke everybody up. It made people more aware that major disasters can hap-pen and need good management.

According to those who

The extraordinary scene at the Staines by-pass: note the Toni ice-cream van providing refreshments for what the newspapers called 'the ghouls'.

had rehearsed a disaster plan for Heathrow not long before the accident, the assumption had been that a crash would happen actually on the airport, not near to it. The Staines disaster made David Sadler think about what would have happened had an aircraft crashed into one of the reservoirs or gravel pits around Heathrow. He set up meetings with the ambulance service and local fire brigades to plan for that eventuality.

Yet however much planning and rehearsing there is, emotions always run high at disasters. The reality is a shock for nearly everybody, trained rescue worker and bystander alike. Plans will never determine who arrives at the site first, or what happens in the next fifteen minutes, nor can the most rigid and disciplined of regimes eliminate the impulse of nearly everyone to save lives rather than organize.

Colin Meek, who went on to become Surrey Ambulance Service's director of operations, was a nineteen-year-old ambulanceman at the time of the Staines crash. In 1991 he left the ambulance service and set up his own consultancy in emergency planning, advising large industries and third-world countries. He believes the calibre of emergency workers and their managers was much lower in the 1970s than now. He still remembers the call he received over the radio on 18 June 1972. 'Alongside the A30 at Staines there's some kind of aircraft accident – perhaps a light aircraft.' was followed a minute later by: 'This is a major accident – commercial airliner.'

We set off, but en route we got another call asking us to a go to road traffic accident nearby, where a child was hurt. We diverted there, and the girl was almost completely uninjured – it was just a scratch. Nevertheless we were ordered to take her to hospital, so we dropped her off before heading for Staines.

By now the radio was saying it was catastrophic and virtually everything was being sent. As we got closer we hit the jams. The traffic was gridlocked. I had to get out and literally tell motorists where to move their cars. At one point I drove

right over the middle of a grassed roundabout. When we arrived there were already twenty ambulances on the bypass, from Surrey, Bucks, London, Herts, and St Johns. We were told to stay with the other vehicles but decided not to and drove round in convoys to the other side of the field. After we got there fire broke out on the aircraft.

A British Airports Authority fire tender had turned up with cutting gear which generated sparks as it sliced through the metal. This started a considerable fire while rescue workers were still in the fuselage. Fortunately, it was put out with foam. 'A whistle was blown and everybody ran for their lives,' Meek recalls. 'We jumped into our ambulance and drove off at high speed across the field.'

Meek took the bodies of two adults and two children to a hangar at Heathrow which had been set up as a temporary mortuary. 'It was one of the most difficult things I've had to do in my life. There were upwards of ninety bodies in there, and it was so harrowing I could not look at them. That's when the scale of it hit me. What was remarkable, unnerving, was why so many died in that impact. Were the G-forces really so big as to kill everybody?'

The sightseers who were such a disturbing and potentially disastrous feature at Staines angered many rescue workers. Some remember police shouting 'Ghouls!' at the crowds through their loud-hailers. But the inquisitive continued to arrive at Staines long after any hope of rescue had gone, hampering the grim work of collecting evidence and the bodies of the crash victims. They were still proving a nuisance days afterwards. Ozzie Healey, who was a sergeant at Staines Police Station at the time, did not go to the crash site himself, but remembers the sightseers only too well. He has a sad postscript to the story.

People were coming from miles around in their cars and on foot and they wouldn't leave. They came every hour of the day and night and for days afterwards. We were sick and tired of them. One man came in a few days after the crash and asked where the site was. I exploded at him. 'You ghoul!' I shouted. He burst into tears and told me one of the air hostesses had been his fiancée. I felt terrible.

Although there were no survivors to be rescued and treated at Staines there was still a great deal to organize in terms of identifying bodies, certifying causes of death, coping with the bereaved and ferrying dignitaries to and from the site. These duties, which do not form part of the rescue operation itself, can nonetheless overlap with it and cause problems at disasters where there are a number of survivors. Handling the distressed calls of victims' relatives and friends can threaten the communication channels of emergency services, jamming lines and tying up manpower. This is truer today than it was in the Seventies, when news travelled more slowly and communications in general were poorer. And even the most sophisticated equipment, the cellphones and modern radio communications, can collapse under the weight of the desperate need for news.

Since 1972, there have fortunately been very few major air crashes in Britain itself. Most planes which came down with British people on board have crashed in other countries, and have therefore not tested the rescue work of our emergency services. In some, notably the Lockerbie disaster, there was no hope of any survivors, except among victims on the ground. There is only one air disaster which invites comparison with Staines.

Just under seventeen years after the Trident crash, on another Sunday, this time in midwinter, another airliner, with 126 passengers and crew on board, was in trouble close to a busy road. This was not a repeat of the Staines disaster, for the pilot had radioed that the plane was in difficulty. In this case that fact was also apparent to the passengers, who could see that one of the engines was on fire – an observation that, remarkably, nobody passed on to the flight crew, who knew only from a sudden series of vibrations that something was wrong. They saw and smelled the smoke, but could not get a clear indication from their instrument panel of what precisely was wrong.

The plane was a Boeing 737, built the previous year, which had notched up only 520 flying hours when it took off from London's Heathrow Airport on 8 January 1989 on a regular shuttle flight to Belfast. It took to the air at about 7.50pm and climbed to 6,000ft, where it levelled off. About a quarter of an hour later, as it climbed to its cruising altitude of around 28,000ft, the crew noticed the vibrations and a smell of smoke. The commander took over, switched off the autopilot and tried to diagnose the problem. He radioed London Air Traffic Control that he had an emergency, though they were not sure at this stage whether it was the left or the right engine that was giving trouble.

It was a bizarre and ultimately tragic state of affairs. The first officer, asked by the commander which engine was playing up, at first said it was the left one, the number 1 engine, then changed his mind and said the right engine (number 2). The number 2 engine was throttled back and for a moment the problem seemed to have been resolved. But the commander did not know that some passengers and the cabin attendants could see sparks coming from the left engine. The commander called in the flight service manager and asked him if he had seen smoke, to which he replied that he had. He was told to pack up the cabin and put everything away. Shortly afterwards the flight service manager went back to the cockpit to say that the passengers were becoming alarmed and panicky. To reassure them, the commander announced that there was trouble with the right engine, which had produced some smoke in the cabin; that it had been shut down; and that they would be landing at East Midlands Airport in about ten minutes.

Some of the passengers thought this odd as they had seen fire in the left not the right engine, but later the cabin crew, who had seen the same thing, said they had not noticed the discrepancy. Nobody said anything to the commander, who could not see the engines himself from the cockpit.

When the Boeing 737 dropped to 2,000ft to make an emergency landing at East Midlands Airport, coming in over the M1 motorway near the village of Kegworth, the emergency services had already been alerted. The airport fire crews waited and watched; the fire brigade took up their positions in anticipation of a crash, as did the ambulance services. Although they were fully prepared, nobody expected anything dramatic to happen, because at this stage nobody realized the true peril the plane was in. The 737 was designed to fly on one engine and there was no reason to believe it would not make it to the airport, dropping low over the M1 before touching down.

Gerald Hofman, a sub-officer with the East Midlands Airport Fire Service, explains.

The wreckage of the Boeing 737 on the M1 near Kegworth. Miraculously it skidded across six lanes of the motorway without hitting any vehicles.

At 8.05pm Air Traffic Control phoned to say that an aircraft leaving Heathrow had an engine problem and was diverting to East Midlands. This was pretty run-of-the-mill – over a year you might get two dozen of these calls, and it's not unusual for a plane to have to shut down one engine.

I notified the crew and we estimated its time of arrival at around 20.25pm. We finished our tea. At this stage we weren't excited. At 20.20 we manned the vehicle and sat on the station forecourt as the aircraft approached. We were dependent at this stage on information from the captain of the aircraft. An emergency was declared and we contacted the local authority fire brigade, but we were still pretty laid back. We were considering how to tackle potential problems. We

decided to cover the landing from two main points on the airfield. We saw the aircraft's lights approaching. It seemed a bit slow, but it was only operating on one engine so that was normal. We still weren't getting excited. But as he got closer I saw burning material falling from the engine of the plane, and I knew that at least one of them was on fire. It was still four or five miles away at this point.

The ambulances and fire and police vehicles had gathered at agreed rendezvous points to await news from Air Traffic Control. They could not see the stricken Boeing, and for most of the rescue workers this was still no more than a routine alert. The Leicestershire Police might get sixty or seventy emergency reports from the airport a year, more than one a week, and this one seemed nothing out of the ordinary.

It was not the emergency services but the crew and passengers on the plane and the people living in the village of Kegworth who knew first that the plane was going to crash. The flight crew must have seen below them, too close, the busy M1 motorway and, just beyond, the lights of the runway. Many people in Kegworth heard the banging of the Boeing's engine and went out into their gardens to look. They knew this was not a normal landing. They had often expressed the fear that sooner or later a plane would come down on them. This Boeing 737 very nearly did.

David Jones, a forty-three-year-old mechanical engineer and chairman of Kegworth Parish Council, was relaxing at home.

We were just sitting down eating supper before putting the children to bed when we heard this terrible banging sound, a kind of 'boom, boom,' and I thought it was maybe a lorry on the motorway with a puncture. I got up and went to the window and saw this plane coming down. I said to the wife, 'You won't believe this.' We could see it was in trouble – there was fire in one of the engines – and we went out into the garden and watched it go over the horizon. We weren't sure if it had made it to the airport or not, but the giveaway was that we heard no reverse thrust. We are used to hearing that when a plane lands.

David Jones phoned someone else in the village to ask if the plane had come down, and was told that it had apparently cleared the houses. Then he took a call from another villager who had seen where the plane had crashed. For a while he sat and thought about what he should do.

The 1980s had been a bad few years for disasters, and in your mind you remember all these stories about people hampering the work of the emergency services. I was not sure whether to go or not. But in the end I felt I just had to go in case there was anything I could do – I did have a first-aid certificate. Because I did not want to get in the way of the emergency services I did not take the car. I went on my bike, through all the little back streets. I went on to the motorway bridge where there was a crowd looking down at the crash.

The Boeing had lost power before it made the runway. Its tail section had scraped the ground just before the motorway, and it had then skidded across all six lanes of traffic, both north and southbound, hit the central reservation with its undercarriage, and smashed into the steep, wooded embankment on the west side of the M1. The nose rose into the air and the tail snapped and folded upwards, and then the plane slid back and came to rest, one engine still on fire. Astonishingly, not one vehicle on the motorway was hit, and the traffic managed to stop without any serious accidents.

A matter of seconds after the crash, Lesley Pendleton was crossing the road over the M1 having collected her daughter to take her home to Kegworth. She did not see the plane come down, but saw the wreckage maybe fifteen seconds after the impact. 'I stopped the car on the bridge,' she recalls. 'It was very eerie. The M1 was full of cars, coaches and lorries, and everyone seemed to open their doors simultaneously. Everything was quiet, the traffic just stopped. There were firemen there within minutes.'

As Lesley Pendleton got back into her car and drove back to Kegworth to break the news, Gerald Hofman and his fire crew at the airport were arriving. He remembers the agonizing moments when they realized the plane had crashed.

I saw the lights dip and I thought, 'He's a bit short.' Then he dipped out of sight, and again I thought, 'He's short – how short? He will slide up the runway.' As the plane vanished there was a void of time that seemed to last forever – it was probably just a few moments. I was still waiting for the plane to come back into sight. I was thinking, 'He can't have hit the deck, he has not exploded. He's gone down, the damn thing is down . . .'

The crews of the three fire engines had to decide what to do. Two of the engines carried foam and the third, a lighter one, had water. 'At this stage,' says Hofman, 'we were not sure where the plane was, but I thought it was on the motorway – that was our first bit of luck.' The lighter engine went off on the A453 which runs behind the motorway embankment where the plane had come down, and the other two set off down the runway. Hofman got on to the southbound carriage of the motorway, the furthest from the plane, and sprayed foam across three lanes. 'This did not put the fire out, but it contained it,' he says. 'The more focused hoses from other tenders put it out.'

It is estimated that the airport fire crew had reached the burning wreckage within two minutes and thirty-eight seconds. 'I thought there would be no rescue work unless we knocked that fire out,' Hofman says. 'The whole lot would fry. Aviation fuel takes forty-five seconds to reach 800 degrees Centigrade from ignition. The fuselage would have burned at 600 degrees, so you don't have long. If the plane had been three or four miles away there would have been no chance of a rescue. *Where the plane landed by the motorway was our second bit of luck.'* The position of the Boeing made it easy to reach with the hoses from both the motorway and the A453.

A minute or so after spraying the aircraft, Hofman went up to the wreckage and became involved in the rescue. 'We could hear banging from the tail of the aircraft. Another fireman opened the door and a cabin crew member literally fell out. He was conscious but badly injured.' There were already many walking wounded climbing out of the wreckage.

Gareth Jones was a passenger on the plane. He describes the crash.

We knew we were being diverted to East Midlands Airport and we thought we were going to make it. About seven seconds before we hit, the skipper said, *'Brace for a crash,' and then we knew. I felt great concern and I just thought, this is it, it's curtains, it's all over. The lady next to me would not get down into a brace position and by the time I had got her to brace we had hit. The first impact was when the tail hit the field. It felt like a fairly moderate bump in a car. I looked up the central aisle and the lights were still on, but I saw them oscillate and I thought again, 'This is it.' For all I knew we were still in the air. I could see sparks coming out of the engine. I passed out for four or five seconds and when I came to we were at rest. I could see a burning bush and it was obvious we had crashed, we had come down.*

Jones had been told at Heathrow to read the emergency procedure before the plane took off because he was sitting next to an emergency exit. When he came round he remembered the instructions.

I took my seat belt off and went through the emergency door. I remembered the Manchester incident [1985] and about the fire coming in and it concentrated my mind. I dragged the woman next to me out and then I went back to help. I could only see the middle section of the plane, and there were firemen in there. I could see dead people and others struggling to get out. I remember a fireman telling me to bugger off as I tried to get into the wreckage. 'You are not doing any good in here,' he said. As soon as I saw the uniforms my adrenaline went and I made my way back down to the hard shoulder and collapsed. As I lay there, I took in the whole scene. People on the motorway had stopped and one woman came up to me and took my phone number and rang my wife to say that I was OK. There were motorists bringing blankets, firemen trying to get people out of the plane and ambulancemen assessing the injured. The ambulancemen came to me. I knew I was not badly hurt so they left me to deal with people who were worse. But they kept

A human chain, including many members of the public, was formed to help pass the dead and injured from the wreckage of the Boeing, which had snapped in half on the motorway embankment.

A message came over the car radio about an aircraft in trouble and I was asked to go to the emergency rendezvous point at East Midlands Airport. We sometimes got these calls once or twice a week. They asked me to tune into the emergency channel. I was on my own and travelling at 90mph so I couldn't, but I knew something was happening when they asked me to do that. When I was about a mile from the scene I came across stationary traffic on the motorway. I had just left a road accident and I thought, 'Oh God, not another crash.' I made my way through about twenty cars and a coach skewed across the road. There were people looking a bit white-faced and I thought this was a bit iffy. Then, as I got in front of the traffic the plane slid down the embankment towards me, still on fire. There were people falling out. I did not feel panic but excitement – the adrenaline leaped to my throat.

Bob Salter joined other policemen at the scene in trying to kick in exit doors and get survivors away from the burning plane. He was covered in foam, and people were sliding down the embankment. 'My main problem was containing the incident, although I did go to rescue passengers. Members of the public had got out of their cars, the whole kit and caboodle were there, vicars and priests and officers started arriving from other counties and we found ourselves swamped with personnel.'

Salter put three survivors in the back of his Range Rover and got on the radio. 'I tried to paint a picture of the situation for Control,' he explains. 'I was the incident officer because no senior officer arrived for forty-five minutes. So I had to manage it and keep tabs on the motorway. The crash was publicized immediately so one minute nobody was there

coming back to me and it was only when I began to shiver – I was wet through with foam and it was January – that they could see the shock was setting in. They packed me off to Queens Medical Centre in Nottingham in an ambulance.

Gareth Jones had torn ligaments and broken ribs, but he was back home after two days in hospital, and full of admiration for the emergency services.

At the time the plane went down, Bob Salter, who was training as a major incident officer, was a motorway police sergeant on patrol duty.

and the next everybody wanted to have a look. But the A453 was closed off so members of the public could not drive to the scene.' Although motorists, AA men and local people did get involved in the Kegworth rescue operation, there was no repeat of the sightseeing scenes at Staines in 1972. Communication between the first police, ambulance crews and firefighters to arrive and their respective control centres was much swifter. And though the operation had to be controlled by rescue workers who temporarily assumed the responsibilities of incident officers before more senior people arrived, they did have an idea of what their role should be.

Police first sealed off the southbound carriageway of the motorway with cones at the nearest junction, but it could not be closed to all traffic until the ambulances and fire engines that were arriving in enormous numbers from three adjoining counties had got through. Eventually the traffic halted by the plane crash was turned back, and the local authority helped by ripping up the central barrier to make it easier for vehicles to turn round.

The broad, hard surface of the motorway was ideal for the emergency services as it gave them room to organize and manoeuvre; a field, for example, would have created much greater problems. But the crash site itself, a steep wooded slope, and the conditions of a damp winter's night exacerbated by the slippery foam everywhere, made the rescue operation extremely difficult. Walter Richardson, then deputy chief ambulance officer for Leicester, was off duty and on his way home when he heard on the radio about the crash. He went straight to the scene, and as it turned out, he was the first ambulanceman to arrive, even though he was not one of those who had been alerted to a possible disaster as part of the emergency plan. All such plans tend to assume that the designated incident officer will arrive to mastermind the rescue operation from the outset, but as we have seen this rarely happens in practice, so the first person there needs to take on this role in the first hectic minutes.

Richardson realized he had to take charge for the ambulance service. 'It was the first time in twenty-five years on the job that I walked away from injured people, but if I had gone to people I would have lost the incident from the managerial point of view,' he explains. 'Within the first thirty seconds I requested "Make ambulances forty with another ten standing by." I asked for my chief to go to the control room before I knew how bad it was going to be – it was a gut reaction.' By involving his most senior officer, Richardson had signalled that this was a major accident before he knew the true scale of it himself.

Ambulanceman James Gough from Derby was among the crews awaiting the plane after the emergency alert. Like their colleagues in the fire brigade, he and paramedic Maurice Foster thought the whole thing would be routine until they heard that the plane was down on the motorway just a few yards away from them. 'Nothing prepares you for something like this,' he says. 'When I got there the fire brigade and police had arrived and I looked around for other blue lights – you report to whoever is there before you. Then you find out you are the first.' Gough found Walter Richardson, however, who handed him a clipboard and pen and told him to get cracking. Inside Gough's cap was an emergency procedure card. He took off the cap and read the instructions: recce the scene, establish a casualty clearing area, and so on. He began to set up a clearing station.

Paramedic Maurice Foster, who was with him, recalls: 'There it was, smoking. I was aghast. "This is real, this is real," I kept on saying to myself. I did not realize how big a plane was. I was gobsmacked.' James Gough and Maurice Foster gathered together and treated some of the passengers who had been pulled from the aircraft. They had plenty of support, as Foster recounts.

Two young chaps came up to me and asked, 'Can we help?' I said, 'That depends,' and asked them who they were. They said they were medical students from Sheffield. Then this other guy comes up to me and says, 'I am an anaesthetist, can I help?' So I said: 'You are the very man.' Then a paramedic from London appeared and I had all this help. We went round and checked the casualties and they all needed treatment, drips and stabilizing. I gave fluids to the medical students and said, 'You will just have to make a decision about who gets what.'

Foster radioed for more fluid and blankets and then someone called from the wreckage for a paramedic and he went into the plane, cutting his foot on some jagged metal which sliced through his boot. He took care of two passengers trapped in the wreckage.

All this frantic activity, the arrival of the East Midlands Airport Fire Service crews, the first police and ambulance workers on the scene, the involvement of motorists and other members of the public, had happened in a matter of minutes. An enormous army of rescue workers was racing to the scene from three counties and beyond, and three hospitals had been alerted – some doctors heard about it first from the TV news – and had sent out teams of flying squads. Senior fire and police officers were also on their way to take charge of the operation.

As always, by the time they got there and the great mêlée of activity was brought into reasonable organization, a great deal had already taken place which bore absolutely no resemblance to the airport master disaster plan. It was not necessarily wrong for all that, and a kind of makeshift, impromptu order was created, much of it through the common sense of people with no emergency-plan training at all. It was perhaps twenty minutes or more after the crash before David Jones from Kegworth arrived on the motorway bridge, still concerned that if he went to help he might be in the way. 'We could see that ambulancemen were having trouble getting casualties out of the nose of the aircraft, because the slope was steep and muddy and they were taking stretchers up to the A453 above.' In effect, the rescue operation had split into two, with casualties from the back of the plane being brought to the motorway, and those from the front going up and over a

fence. In the end, David Jones decided he might be able to be of use.

I found a friend from the village who also had a first-aid certificate and we went down to see what we could do. The first thing we noticed was that the ambulancemen were having difficulties getting the stretchers over a fence about 3ft high, so a group of us leaned on it until we knocked down a section about 30ft to 40ft long.

Then we went down through a dense thicket to where doctors, ambulancemen and firefighters were getting people out of the plane. The ambulancemen were struggling: they did not have enough stretchers, and two of them were carrying casualties up the slope. So we formed a kind of human chain, a walkway from the plane up to where the ambulances were. There must have been about thirty of us, some from the village, motorists and other members of the public. It helped the ambulancemen to see where they were going, and we helped if they were in difficulty. They just did not have enough personnel.

I was at the end of this chain of people, next to the plane. When we were taking folks off it there were so few stretchers that we were moving the bodies on ladders. I can remember the doctor saying, 'There is nothing we can do for this one,' and it would be a ladder. There were people coming out with missing arms and legs, but they were still alive. One man in a suit was passed out and he was immaculate – he looked as if nothing had happened to him at all – but the doctor said he was dead. We could not believe it. I'll never get over that. I had never seen a dead body except when my father died. I went down to look at this man, several of us did, because we just could not believe he was dead. But he was.

From time to time Jones went into the plane to help clear debris which was in the way, and to pull off awkward bits of metal. After about twenty minutes the flow of dead and injured emerging from the plane slowed down, and the corridor of Kegworth villagers and other helpers began to disband. Although David Jones had been nervous about going in, both because he didn't want to be in the way and because he had no stomach for horrible injuries, he says, 'Nobody told me to go away. I expected it, but it didn't happen.' He stayed until about 11pm, helping where he could, always worried that the plane would catch fire and explode and they might all be killed. He says he saw very few policemen and he was never challenged. As he passed the dead and injured laid out by the road on his way back to Kegworth, he did meet a few 'ghouls' – families with young children just going to look. It surprised him that there were no police to turn them back. The rescue operation restored Jones' faith in human nature and made a deep impression on him – he was in tears for several days afterwards.

Among the unofficial helpers were some AA men who happened to be near the crash site and went to see what they could do. Vic Milner, who was on patrol waiting for a breakdown call-out, heard about the crash on his radio. 'A motorbike policeman tried to stop me going to the plane but I just drove straight past. I asked somebody in charge, "What do you want me to do?" and he said, "Just get stuck in."'

Mick Rooney arrived about twenty minutes after the crash and met up with some AA colleagues who were wondering what to do. They got involved in the same rescue operation as David Jones at the front of the plane.

There was a mortuary and ambulances by the roadside but the plane was proving difficult to get to because of all the bushes so I got an axe from a fire officer and cut a path. I helped take the pilot out. He was very badly hurt and in a great deal of pain. He caught his hip on the side of the aircraft as they pulled him out and he screamed. I could feel the pain myself. They thought the tail section of the plane might fall over, so we went over and secured it.

Kegworth drew in a most extraordinary range of unofficial helpers, including a passing mountain-rescue team, who helped to cut steps in the muddy embankment so that rescue workers could get up and down more easily. The part they played was for a time important, but in the context of an enormous operation which at its height involved 700 emergency-service workers, including 181 ambulancemen, it was small. Afterwards some official concern was expressed that the site had not been sealed off as effectively as it could have been. In his report in a special disaster memorial publication, Leicestershire Chief Ambulance Officer Alan Parker picked out as the last of ten lessons learned at Kegworth 'The need for good site control. We had too many ad hoc doctors, ambulance staff, mountain rescue, etc., including members of the public who gained unchallenged access. This requires close police-ambulance co-operation and communications.'

There were stories of bogus doctors who had to be evicted from the site: who they were nobody knows, though the press are the chief suspects. The flying squads from the three hospitals had no special clothing to identify themselves, and there were occasions when doctors were asking AA patrolmen who shouldn't even have been there what they should do. As the crash site was on the borders of three counties, it was not clear which fire brigade was primarily responsible, though the firefighters themselves appear to have worked well together despite problems with equipment – the cutters they had would not penetrate the metal of the wreckage.

The Leicestershire ambulance control vehicle, which should have been the nerve centre of medical communications between the site and the hospitals, was out of action, having blown up on its way to the scene. The first casualty clearing station set up simply disappeared in the melée as ambulances turned up and whisked the wounded off to hospital. Why this happened is not clear. One theory is that there was no need to treat the casualties at the site when they could be quickly taken to hospital; another that the area was overrun with rescue workers and classification and labelling of casualties became impossible. A third attributes its disappearance to the risk of fire or noxious fumes as 17,000 gallons of aviation fuel leaked from the wreckage.

Because the rescue operation split, for good practical reasons, between the front of the aircraft, from which casualties went up to the A453, and the middle and back, from which they went down to the M1, there was, in effect,

Incredibly, more than half the 126 passengers and crew aboard the Boeing survived the crash which hurled seats into a pile inside the plane.

no single site medical officer as in theory there should have been.

Doctors at the site found it very difficult to fill in triage labels because of the foam and the damp night. Pencils just would not write. One hospital forgot to send the labels used to note down injuries and medication given and the rescue workers had to use discarded luggage tags from the wreckage. The two other hospitals had a very different colour-coding system; green meant dead in one triage system and walking wounded in another. Many of the first twenty casualties whisked away did not get the on-site medical help they should have received, according to the disaster plans, and they arrived at the hospitals untreated and un-labelled. Later on, as a proper casualty clearing station was set up, things went much more smoothly. But labels still had to be checked.

As news of the disaster spread, the pressure on hospitals, ambulance services, social services and police casualty centres grew like the waves of an earth tremor. Telephone lines were jammed with calls from the world's media and press conferences had to be held. Various dignitaries who wanted to come to the scene had to be dissuaded because of the confusion and security problems such visits would cause. The traffic built up, and, as David Jones describes it, the village of Kegworth was 'like World War Three' as helicopters, the army and hordes of journalists invaded.

At the heart of all this was the rescue operation itself, as those confronted with the awfulness of a wrecked airliner full of people dead, dying and torn to pieces tempered the first rush of adrenaline with what they had learned in training, adrenaline with what they had learned in training, professionalism and powerful human impulses competing inside them. Walter Richardson, the off-duty deputy chief ambulance officer who took charge, remembers:

The first dead body I saw was that of a child, a nine-year-old boy. He was brought to me in the arms of an ambulanceman who asked, 'Where do I put this casualty?' I asked if he had been certified dead and the guy said he had. I told him to put the boy 200 yards up on the hard shoulder. You should have seen the look in his eyes. 'You callous bastard', he said. I reflected about it afterwards and the guy even apologized, but I think I made the right decision. The living come first, and I could not tie up ambulances to move the deceased. But it was a hard one to call.

Each of the emergency services, and the hospital accident and emergency services, accepted enormous public acclaim for their rescue work at Kegworth, but at the same time they all took pains to analyze and criticize their own performance. They made public some of their recommendations and lessons they had learned, and confined others to specialist journals and internal postmortems. If another such crash happens again they will, they hope, be better prepared. But they do not know if they will ever have to deal with anything like the Kegworth disaster again. What they do know is that someone will, somewhere, and that writing up their own experiences will add to the great store of knowledge about the myriad things that can, and do, go wrong when the best-laid plans are put to the test.

To some extent the history of planning for disasters is about the same lessons being learned over and over again. But between Staines in 1972 and Kegworth in 1989 there has been immense change, much of it subtle and beyond the understanding of anyone outside the emergency services. It has to do with a slow but continuous improvement in the training of rescue workers and an acceptance that

emergencies require the use of special skills as well as an elaborate system of communications between all services.

At Kegworth walkie-talkie and cellphone communications broke down at the site because of the number of people trying to talk to each other and the piercing noise of the firefighters' cutting gear as they freed the passengers. The police, fire brigade, ambulance crews and hospital flying squads all used old-time runners to carry information at one time or another, and in the end, the communications problems did not materially affect the success of the operation.

Of the 126 people on board the ill-fated Boeing, 118 passengers and eight crew, seventy-nine survived, although a great many of them had severe injuries and between them they suffered more than 300 identifiable serious fractures and other critical wounds. Yet Kegworth showed that plane crashes need not be fatal for all on board, and a great deal of research has since been carried out on the nature of 'survivability'. Of those who died, thirty-nine did not survive long enough to benefit from medical treatment, four died the same day in hospital accident and emergency departments and four a few days later.

A study of the nature of the injuries of both victims and survivors using hospital records, which scored the severity of damage on an established standard scale, suggested that only thirteen passengers were properly speaking 'walking wounded' and able to help in their own rescue. All the rest would probably have died had the emergency services not arrived so swiftly to free them from the wreckage and treat them. And there might have been no survivors at all if the fire crews had not got there as quickly as they did and the Boeing had been engulfed in flames as the burning engine ignited leaking fuel.

Although firefighters did use foam to contain the blaze, the time-honoured method of dousing the flames with water did the trick. And it is to the history of firefighting in the much more difficult conditions of smoke-filled buildings that we move on.

Chapter Four
SMOKE-EATERS

At just after 2.15am on 23 January 1958, Clerkenwell Fire Station in London – now the world's oldest operational station – received a 999 call from a cold-storage firm in Smithfield Market to say that a fire had broken out. To be called out by telephone was then still a novelty for the London Fire Brigade, for it was only in the previous year that their chief, Frederick Delve, had arranged with the Post Office a system of free 999 calls for the fire, police and ambulance services.

Before that the fire brigade had been alerted by street alarms, which involved smashing a glass panel to pull a brass handle and transmit a message to the fire station. These had been taken out of action during the war and reinstated after it, but false alarms had been running at about 95 per cent as the temptation to break the glass without waiting for a fire was

Flames burst through from the basement of the poultry market in Smithfield, London, in 1958. Despite the efforts of 1,700 firemen, the building was razed to the ground.

Fire crews heading down into the labyrinth of tunnels under Smithfield, wearing the old proto-oxygen breathing-apparatus sets.

were favoured as firemen because of their knowledge of ropes and their fitness and discipline. They were brave, too, as all firemen have to be, and prided themselves on their ability to take punishment in a fire – the toughest were dubbed 'smoke-eaters' and could 'chew smoke'. There was a bravado and a disdain for modern equipment: fire-fighting was a daring business, an art of sense, touch, instinct and experience. And indeed, although there have been many changes between the 1950s and the pre-sent day – new kinds of breathing apparatus and safeguards for their use, better protective clothing and far greater concern for the firefighters' safety – the way in which fires are tackled has remained fundamentally the same. It is still dangerous, and it requires real daring to go in behind the hose to douse the flames with water.

The men who tackled the Smithfield fire still drilled in the old way at fire stations, all of which had towers in their parade yards, the original purpose of which was to hang up the 75ft-long hoses to dry because the canvas material covering them became water-logged when they were used, making them heavy and causing the rubber lining to rot. Firemen then did a regular morning and afternoon drill from the tower, which was a bit like a circus act and often drew a crowd of interested onlookers. There was the wheeled-ladder and hook-ladder performance, in which

clearly too great for many people to resist.

The crew who hit the bells and jumped on to the pump escape that morning were in many ways a different breed of firefighters from those in the service today. A large number were ex-servicemen, particularly from the navy, who the escape was pushed to the tower, a fireman went up and fixed another ladder to it, and then a second fireman went over him with a hook ladder, attaching it to a window ledge and climbing to the top. The chief, Freddy Delve, was keen on fitness and daring. He insisted on games in the drill yard, and on one particular exercise which involved firemen lowering a man of their own weight from a rope on the tower. The guinea pig had to tie a 'chair knot' and entrust his own life to it as he was lowered to the ground. It looked pretty spectacular, and indeed it struck the fire brigade's union as an exercise generally more hazardous than the real business of fighting fires. The union opposed it for years, even taking the issue to the High Court, where they lost. They had to wait until Delve retired in 1962 before some of the old drills disappeared, but the wheeled escape and the hook ladder survived until 1979.

Practising the use of breathing apparatus in smoke was another routine exercise, and it was this skill, rather than those honed by the ladder or 'chair-knot' drill, which was to prove critical in fighting the Smithfield fire. The brigade had had breathing apparatus of some kind since the 1840s, when a gift was made by the Paris fire brigade of an outfit that looked a bit like frogman's gear to James Braidwood, superintendent of the London fire-engine establishment. In the 1950s they had a slightly comical-looking arrangement involving corrugated tubing and two oxygen cylinders. These breathing-apparatus (BA for short) sets were not carried on all fire engines, but they could be called for if a fire was particularly smoky or deep-seated.

Only five minutes after the 999 call, the first Clerkenwell fire engine reached Smithfield. The crew were shown into the basement of the poultry market by the Union Cold Storage Company. Station Officer Jack Fourt-Wells arrived and went down into the labyrinth of tunnels, where there was thick smoke. Nobody knew where the fire itself was but by now the smoke was filling all the tunnels containing carcasses and poultry so that a search had to be

made in these catacombs in almost total blindness. Station Officer Fourt-Wells, a forty-six-year-old married man with two children and twenty years' experience in the brigade, put on his BA set and went back down into the maze of tunnels. It was thought that the fire might be in a padlocked cold store, and a key was produced and taken to Fourt-Wells. There was a good deal of this coming and going and after a while Dick Stocking, a thirty-one-year-old fireman, also married, with an eleven-year-old daughter, joined Fourt-Wells in the search for the source of the fire.

The proto-oxygen breathing apparatus the firemen had would last an hour, but it could be made to work for a good deal longer by an experienced man who kept calm and did not breathe too hard. When their apparatus was nearing expiry Fourt-Wells sent two firemen back to the street, where crews had been arriving from other stations. But he and Dick Stocking stayed in the tunnels and continued their search.

Bill Ranson, one of 1,700 firemen who, over the next three days, attempted to put out the fire hidden deep beneath Smithfield, describes the breathing apparatus worn by Fourt-Wells and Stocking.

You had a nose clip and a mouthpiece. You could not speak, only grunt. You also had what was called a CEAG lamp [certified electrically against gas], similar to a miner's. If the smoke was thick you began to think, 'Have I got enough oxygen?' and you'd take the pressure gauge out of its pocket and thump on your BA set, and keep looking to see how much oxygen you had left. Normally you could shine a torch on to it, but down there you had to put it up to the eye. You had a pair of goggles in which you were sweating with the heat, and you could hardly see anything.

In those days the use of breathing apparatus was regarded as a specialist skill, so as the smoke intensified and the fire took a firm hold, men with BA experience were called up from other fire stations across London. In the first wave was a crew from Whitefriars Station near Fleet Street with Acting Station Officer John Bishop in charge. An ex-navy man, Bishop had been a docker when his mother saw an advertisement in the paper for firemen. He was the only one of seventeen applicants to get a job. He had trained at Clerkenwell and knew Fourt-Wells. As the reinforcements were going down into the basement to search the tunnels, someone said, 'I wonder where Dick Stocking is?' John Bishop takes up the story.

There was still no sign of flames, just lots of smoke, but conditions were getting worse. It was a maze and we used clapping signals. I was going down the centre and I'd send the men down a passageway here or there. You would walk along one step at a time, with the back of your hand in front of you in case you walked into something red-hot, making sure you were not going to fall down a hole. All we could find was passageways with meat packed on either side from floor to ceiling. The smoke got thicker – you could eat it: black oily smoke. It was very cold down there and you were cold, even though you were sweating. That was fear.

All of a sudden I heard a shout. 'I've got one!' When we got there they'd found Fourt-Wells. I didn't see him until they were pulling him out. But there was no sign of Dick Stocking. I eventually found him. He was lying face-down on the floor and he still had his mouthpiece in and his goggles on – he had run out of oxygen and passed out. I turned him over and dragged him along the floor and the crew came to help. We were carrying him out when all of a sudden I realized I was in trouble myself. I started to feel light-headed and I looked at my gauge. It was empty. We put a line round Dick, dragged him up to the surface and tried resuscitation. From then on it was back to normal firefighting. I was frightened, but calm frightened.

Fourt-Wells and Stocking had got lost and Fourt-Wells, who was one of the old 'smoke-eaters' and would not give up, had been overcome. Dick tried to drag him out. When he couldn't he went back for help, but he must have taken a wrong turning. I think he was trying to dig his way through the meat when he collapsed.

Both Fourt-Wells and Stocking were dead. Fourt-Wells was found among the carcasses with his breathing apparatus ripped off. As the oxygen ran out he would have been breathing in smoke and would have suffocated. One of those who brought him out, at 4.40am, was Ken Birch, a sub-officer on the emergency tender based at Lambeth. Birch had been there early on and at one stage had thought he had found the seat of the fire. But he had gone down without any hoses, and had to go back to get lights and equipment to tackle it. When he returned with reinforcements, what had been glowing was burning more fiercely, and drove them back out again. Then they were ordered to help in the search for the missing firemen. 'I'd just gone down into the basement passages,' Birch recalls, 'when a shout went up that Fourt-Wells' body had been found. Conditions had really deteriorated and I had to help get him out. We put him on this rocking resuscitation stretcher, and I took his belt and axe off and tried to revive him with a Novox resuscitator.'

Ken Birch finished his shift and went home to his wife, telling her that he had been to a serious incident at Smithfield Market but that it had been dealt with. He remembers: 'When we later turned on the news and the headline was "Blazing inferno at Smithfield Meat Market," my wife turned to me and said, "Is that the fire you put out, dear?"'

Whether or not Birch had found the source of the fire before switching his attention to the search for the missing men, it was lost again in the thick smoke that filled the labyrinth of underground passageways. Despite their brave efforts, the firemen never did manage to put out the fire until the entire building had collapsed.

With two firemen dead and the fire taking a

firmer hold, a crew arrived from Kingsland Road Station in Dalston at around 6am. Sub-officer Don Tyler and Eric Gunn were working together – all firemen then, as now, worked with at least one other colleague as a safety measure. Eric Gunn remembers the experience vividly.

> While we were on our way to Smithfield, Don Tyler asked me if I'd been on a decent BA job. He had obviously already realized that conditions were going to be difficult. I said I had, but nothing in my previous experience had prepared me for what lay ahead. The conditions were atrocious. The smoke was so thick that visibility was nil, so trying to make our way through passages stacked with boxes of chicken was very difficult. We were pushing our way forward but none of us really knew where the fire was: I had a terrible

At Smithfield, a check on which crews had gone down at what time was kept on a blackboard, but no record was made of the first firemen who went in. Two of them got lost and died.

> suspicion it was actually behind us.
>
> Not long after we went down into the basement, I remember Don saying that there was something wrong with his BA set. He checked his valves and everything seemed OK, but shortly afterwards he started to giggle, the first sign that he was taking in too much oxygen. Minutes later he collapsed and we had to drag him out with a line.

'Things were very bad,' agrees Don Tyler.

> I couldn't see any flames but the heat was terrific and the smoke was very thick, and

there was this terrible smell because of the burning meat and fat. I obviously didn't know it at the time, but it turned out I was wearing defective equipment. We must have been in the basement for about five or ten minutes when I started to feel woozy. I vaguely recall someone kicking me and the next thing I remember was waking up in hospital – Bart's – hours later.

The famous St Bartholomew's Hospital, now sadly half closed down, is next to Smithfield, near enough for Tyler to have seen the huge flames from his window. 'I asked the nurse which building was on fire and I couldn't believe it when she said "Smithfield Meat Market" – I certainly hadn't expected it to get that serious.'

Although they were tackling an exceptionally difficult fire, the gear they had and the way they worked back in 1958 was no different from usual. However, Eric Gunn and Don Tyler can appreciate how primitive it was. Gunn provides an example.

One of the things I saw at the fire showed why change was needed. At the time the practice was for the 'initial attendance' crews to go in without leaving a record of their names and time of entry. The blackboard system, with names and times chalked up, was not used until four pumps were present. If the firemen failed to return at the expected time an emergency crew would be sent in.

Once Don was safely on his way to hospital, I went back to the basement entrance and, happening to glance at the blackboard, I noticed that the

names of my team had been rubbed off. This hadn't been done intentionally. It had happened by accident during the struggle to get Don out – our bodies must have rubbed off the chalk. It was pure chance that it was our names which had gone: we could just as easily have wiped out the names of our colleagues who were still in the basement. It made me realize that a more thorough system was needed.

Don Tyler adds:

Back then, things were very different. For

The stench of roasting meat pervaded the Smithfield fire; during the three days it burned, many firemen were overcome by the fumes.

example, we never questioned the fact that we didn't have whistles or any other warning systems on our BA sets. BA just wasn't recognized in the same way. For a start, only a few firemen per pump had the apparatus and if you wore it you could be called chicken. If you 'chewed smoke', then you'd be held in very high regard – it was quite the thing to brag about how long you could cope in smoky conditions without wearing BA. Putting all that gear on took time, and when you were anxious to start tackling the fire itself, fiddling around with the straps and putting your goggles in water to try to keep them clear just seemed to take too long. As a sub-officer, even after Smithfield, I remember telling my men off for wasting time putting their BA sets on when they should have been fighting the fire. Looking back, I suppose our attitude and outlook was quite wrong.

Wave upon wave of firemen went into the basement of the poultry market as the heat intensified. The tunnels were mostly lined with cork, which had become impregnated with fat and burned with the thickest, blackest smoke they had ever seen. Crews with BA sets were driven back by the unbearable heat and scrambled for the ladders to the surface. Bill Ranson remembers going down into the smoke with an assistant divisional officer (ADO).

We went down the ladder and fell over because there were three men at the bottom. They'd just collapsed, though they'd still got their BA sets on. Anyway, we got them back up, and then I lost the ADO. In those days ADOs used to wear a kind of chained epaulette on their shoulder. So I'm feeling everybody's shoulder, trying to find out if they're him, and of course, I never did find him until we came out.

In the 1950s the London Fire Brigade had their own mobile canteen, based at Lambeth, to keep the men refreshed at a big fire. The Lambeth canteen duly arrived at Smithfield, but even the short breaks between forays into the burning basement turned out to be far from comfortable, as Ranson relates:

Although you'd been swallowing mouthfuls and

stomachfuls of smoke down there, if you
were a smoker the first thing you did was
light up a cigarette. So we'd get upstairs
and it was icy cold: one minute you're
sweating and warm down there, then you
come up and you start to get cold, the
tunic starts to freeze and an ice lining
forms on your helmet where it has got
wet. We were at the canteen van – I can
see it now – I had a cup of Bovril in a thick,
old-fashioned cup and on the counter was
this glass full of cigarettes.

I said to the chap, 'Whose are these?'
He said, 'Anybody's, mate.' I lit one up
and my colleague lit one up and you took
two drags at it and it disappeared. Players
of Nottingham had sent down some of
their cheap Weights brand to keep the
Smithfield firemen going.

The Smithfield fire was one of the biggest there
had ever been in London. As it spread
underground, more and more crews were
driven back by the heat and smoke until all
men were eventually called out of the
basement. The casualties were escalating at an
alarming rate: as well as the two deaths,
twenty-six firemen, including Don Tyler,
received hospital treatment.

An attempt to flood the fire out by filling the
basement with water failed because it drained
away too quickly, and ultimately the building
began to weaken and groan. It collapsed after
the fire had raged for three days. Market
traders had to move out and squat in other
Smithfield buildings for a long time afterwards.

During the three days of the Smithfield fire, 23
to 25 January, the London Fire Brigade
answered 259 other calls, including a big blaze
at a jam factory in Bermondsey, an even bigger
one in some Poplar warehouses and several
other medium-sized fires. In the days before

Market traders at Smithfield doff their caps as the
funeral cortège for the firemen who died there
passes by.

79

much stricter fire regulations were enforced, there were blazes every day of the week, many more than there are today. Buildings themselves generally had few built-in fire-inhibiting designs, and though a British Fire Prevention Committee had been formed as far back as 1897, brigades did not have the legal powers they have today to enforce regulations.

The single most significant change in the work of the fire brigade since the last war has undoubtedly been in the dull but effective business of fire prevention and in ensuring that those that do start do not get out of control. The success here is one of the reasons that the fire service has been able, and some would say keen – for all brigades indulge in 'empire-building' – to take on more special-service work, such as extrication at road accidents and railway crashes. Outside firefighting pure and simple, there have been remarkable technological developments and new skills learned. But as already noted, and as every firefighter today with experience going back to the 1950s will confirm, firefighting itself has not changed very much since the 1950s.

At first this might seem surprising, because firefighters look so different now. Their old tunics, made of heavy woollen Melton cloth, have been discarded. These tunics were based, according to Sally Holloway, historian of the London Fire Brigade, on the old watermen's livery – the watermen who provided London's passenger transport on the Thames were the first firemen. Lighter, heat-resistant material is now used. The old helmets made of cork were replaced by a new model produced from synthetic materials and designed in New Zealand for the 1990s. But innovation is usually slow in institutions like the fire brigades, which retain a kind of traditional, regimental character and tend to hang on to trusty old gear as long as they can. They are very cautious in

The Smithfield fire was fought in a bitterly cold January: water has frozen to the cork helmet of this young fireman.

trying out new equipment which might reveal hidden and fatal faults, and when they have made up their mind what they want, there is usually a political battle over the cost of updating and renewal.

The history of the firefighter's helmet is a case in point. In London, for example, the first insurance-company brigades in the eighteenth century favoured leather helmets for their firemen, who wore a variety of coloured coats. James Braidwood, who came from Edinburgh to form the first truly professional fire brigade in London in the early nineteenth century, favoured black leather, with the characteristic crest as a defence against falling debris. He also issued firemen with black silk scarves to protect their necks from falling sparks. Today they still have scarves, made of Nomex, a synthetic material.

The leather helmet survived in London until the 1860s, when the Metropolitan Fire Brigade (funded by the old Metropolitan Board of Works, forerunner of the London County Council) was established. Its first chief was Captain Sir Eyre Massey Shaw, a man who wanted to be in charge of the most up-to-date brigade in the world. He redesigned uniforms and made a special study of firemen's helmets in Europe and America. He thought American models were too wide-brimmed and cumbersome, but he was impressed by the streamlined headgear of the Paris *pompiers*, which was strong but light, and allowed firemen through narrow openings. Inspired by these helmets, Shaw had his own designed, which were to be made of brass. The metal itself had no special protective quality, but it looked grand and was a distinctive feature of London firemen until 1936.

Sally Holloway, in her book *Courage High!*, a history of London firefighting, gives an excellent account of the factors Shaw took into consideration in his design.

The new helmet that Shaw designed had a front peak which shaded the eyes without interfering with the vision, a back peak which protected the neck and ears from molten lead from roofs, but was slightly cut away at the ears so that he [the fireman] could still hear without difficulty; a 'comb' on top, strong enough to resist the force of a blow from falling masonry or timber and the pattern intended to make sure that if a man did drop unconscious, his helmet would protect his face and the back of his head whether he fell forward or backward. The dragons embellishing the sides of the crest are said to have been designed by Shaw's daughter Anna. The material, brass, had no function other than to distinguish MFB men from the rest.

Shaw reckoned that leather helmets probably gave as much protection and both were liable to be penetrated by sharp objects such as falling slates. One practical advantage of the brass design was that any section which had been damaged could be easily unscrewed and a new piece screwed back in its place.

The old helmets, too damaged to be reused, were remodelled into miniatures which were used as collection boxes. So that he would stand out at any incident, the chief officer's helmet was silver.

Shaw's meticulous planning provides an insight into the requirements of firefighting then and now. Equipment has to be eminently practical, providing protection while not restricting the firefighter's ability to feel and sense things, and must not hamper him in his work, which always was and remains physically tough, sometimes frightening, but above all exciting. The demise of Shaw's carefully crafted helmet was signalled by the arrival of electricity.

By the 1920s, homes previously lit and heated by gas began to be wired on a large scale, and firemen were in danger of electrocution if a cable fell on their brass helmets. Indeed, in 1925 a sub-officer died in this way, and at the inquest the jury asked the London County Council, then the fire authority, to look into the danger of brass helmets. It did so, only to conclude that this was a danger firemen just had to face; it was all part of the job. After all, they could just as easily be electrocuted through wet clothing or the nozzle of the hosepipe.

It was not until eleven years later, after a year's trial, that a much safer non-metallic helmet was adopted. The manufacturers, Merryweathers, claimed it would withstand a current of 11,000 volts. Their 'super safety helmet' was 'shockproof, waterproof, flameproof, unbreakable and lighter than leather or brass . . . four-ply virgin cork treated to ensure insulation, adhered and insulated with pure rubber solution covered with cotton drill, steeped in non-alkaline, flameproof solution and covered in heat-resisting enamel to withstand a temperature of 350 degrees Fahrenheit without change.' These were the helmets firemen wore until only a few years ago, when the new lighter fibreglass and kevlar helmets with visors were brought in.

It is a common misconception about firefighting that the greatest problem is flame and heat. It isn't: smoke is the major hazard, and most of the serious work is done in almost total blindness. Turk Manning's career as a firefighter based in Soho, London's red-light district and clubland, spanned most of the technological and other changes from the late 1950s until the 1980s. He became a specialist in the use of breathing apparatus as he had to tackle so many basement fires, both in central London and in the docklands, where he was often called out to problem fires in smoke-filled, cavernous basements like those at Smithfield.

The fight is the same; the only thing that changes is the weapons. As for getting lost, when I first joined you were just taught not to. But under firefighting conditions – the noise, the excitement and exhaustion – it is easy to get separated from the hose. You were supposed to hang onto your colleague, but events often overtake you.

I can recall being parted from my colleague in an underground car park. You stop and listen and hear his breathing-apparatus valves clicking. This is what people don't understand from films like The Towering Inferno. *They're just not realistic. You can't see anything at all. It is very difficult for me to talk about tackling a fire, as you can't possibly envisage what it is like. Everybody has the concept that fire is fire, but it isn't. There are so many aspects, and each one is different. It is frightening, but there is the excitement, like motor-racing has for some people, which gives you the buzz.*

The classic image of the fireman atop a ladder where a mother and child await rescue as flames lick at them from a window does happen, but it is probably one of the rarest experiences in a fireman's life. Men like Turk Manning were capable of moving a wheeled escape ladder to a window with well-drilled speed and efficiency, but rescue of this kind was always the exception, and it became even less frequent still when it became common to manufacture household furniture from synthetic material which released highly poisonous gases when it burned. If the brigade did not get there in the first minutes, there was nobody left alive to save.

This toxic smoke also put an end to the bravado of the old smoke-eaters, who might previously have run the gauntlet of the choking clouds coming from a horsehair mattress, dashing in, grabbing someone and dragging him out. The smoke at the Smithfield fire may have been dense and sickly with the fumes of burning poultry, but at least it was not highly toxic. Often the fireman was sick and that was it. And often, even long after Smithfield when breathing apparatus was more generally used by firemen, BA sets were not worn by the first crews in. 'There weren't any BA sets on the first rescue tender – they came along later. So you just went straight in and did your rescue if you could,' says Turk Manning.

By the mid-1970s the frequency with which firemen were faced with poisonous fumes from burning polystyrene tiles, plastics and foams when they went to a fire in a house or office was increasing. In such conditions, even the most ardent smoke-eater could not have

survived for more than a minute. Breathing apparatus was therefore becoming part of the standard kit for every fireman. The old proto-oxygen sets were replaced by compressed-air sets, which were easier to use and much more comfortable. In the oxygen sets the air breathed was recycled through a filter and became very hot. In the compressed-air apparatus it was not recycled, so it remained cool, but the disadvantage was that air did not last as long as it did in the old oxygen sets. There were some other problems, too, with the new equipment, which had a face mask rather than the tube in the mouth, nose clip and separate goggles of the old sets.

The old apparatus was reasonably compatible with beards and side whiskers, which had been ubiquitous in the Victorian era. They went out of fashion around the 1920s, but beards came back with a vengeance in the late 1960s and early 1970s. Unfortunately, they were not compatible with the new compressed-air BA sets. The fire brigade's union did defend those firemen who wanted to retain their facial hair despite the fact that it spoiled the insulation of the BA mask. There has been research into developing a beard-friendly mask but until such a mask becomes a reality, firefighters are not allowed any facial hair that might interfer with their breathing equipment.

Alongside the changes to breathing equipment are other developments, hoses have become lighter, and do not get saturated with water, so they no longer have to be hung up to dry on drill-yard towers. New types of gloves have been developed, too. Experiments have been conducted with thermal-imaging cameras, which enable the user to see through smoke, but to date these have still been too cumbersome in the thick of a fire when speed and agility are essential. In theory, firefighters can now keep in radio contact with the outside world from smoke-filled buildings to prevent them from getting lost, although the equipment does not always function very well underground. Yet each advance in gear tends to take away a little bit of the old-school

The scene above ground at King's Cross tube station in 1987 as a fierce fire raged below in the ticket hall: 31 people, including a firefighter, died.

It is still the strategy of firefighters to get beneath a blaze, because hot air and smoke rise. In a house fire, they will force the door open, take a quick look and go in with their breathing apparatus on, hauling the hose behind them. A fine-spray water curtain helps to keep them cool and if a colleague is in trouble they can play it on him or her. Quickly they are in smoke and darkness, feeling their way, inching along in case a floor has collapsed. Unless the building is one for which they have seen plans and inspected they will know nothing about its layout. They feel walls, listen and move forward, searching for the heart of the fire. It is not until then that the crew can open up with their powerful water jets and knock the fire down. As at Smithfield, finding the fire and judging its potential dangers is the first problem. Fire is treacherous and fickle, and a small, smouldering, inconsequential little bonfire can erupt into a deadly inferno. And, as with so many fires which turn out to be bigger or more catastrophic than anyone could have expected, a nightmare can begin with a call so routine that it creates very little excitement among the first crews to arrive.

At just after 7.30pm on 18 November 1987, a passenger on the London Underground alighted from his train at King's Cross station

fireman's sensitivity. The BA face mask shields the cheeks from heat; with gloves on the firefighter cannot feel a door or a wall to see if it is warm; guidelines attached to him or her in case of disorientation can be an encumbrance if they get tangled or snagged on bits of debris. The old hands will still say that, for all their faults, the proto-oxygen BA sets had their advantages, too. More of their face was exposed so their senses were keener, they could keep the breathing apparatus going longer by being calm and not breathing too hard.

Wearing their modern compressed air-breathing apparatus and protective clothing, a fire crew emerges from one of the King's Cross tube exits.

and mounted the escalator to the ticket hall, which is like a little amphitheatre below the level of the main concourse. Along with another passenger, he saw smoke and a small fire burning under the escalator. A third commuter decided to switch off the escalator with the emergency button. This escalator was one of a set of three together, two going up and the middle one descending. The fire was in the left-hand up-escalator (as seen from below).

Station staff also saw the fire and went into the escalator machine room to turn off the power. One of them got an extinguisher but when he went back to the escalator the fire was getting worse. There were a large number of British Transport Police at King's Cross and nearby Euston, gathered for a special operation that evening. One of them, too, saw the fire from the top of the Piccadilly Line escalator and reported it.

Six minutes after the fire was first noticed by the passengers the London Fire Brigade was called. The nearest station was Euston, but they were already on a call to University College Hospital, so the first engine and crew arrived from Soho. It was at 7.42pm.

What happened in the following five minutes has been told many times, but it remains an almost surreal tragedy, the true cause of which is still a matter of debate. For the small fire burning on the left escalator from the Piccadilly Line flared in seconds into something like a giant blowlamp, blasting into the confined space of the booking concourse and transforming it into a chamber of death. Yet it was only a few feet from the outside world, from the fresh air and the milling crowds of Londoners on their way home or going out for the evening.

When the Soho crew, led by Station Officer Colin Townsley, arrived at King's Cross, there was nothing to indicate that they would be attending one of the worst disasters in the history of the London Underground. Small fires were not unusual on the system, and there had been a big blaze three years earlier at oxford Circus Station, which had filled the tunnels with acrid smoke. Luckily, nobody had

died. Station Officer Townsley went down into the booking hall with three firefighters, leaving two by the engine to await orders.

A minute after the Soho crew, the pump ladder from Clerkenwell arrived with Temporary Sub-Officer Roger Bell in charge. Bell took four firefighters into the station, where they could smell burning. One fireman went back for breathing-apparatus sets while the others took a look at the problem. They could see a small fire burning about a third of the way down the Piccadilly Line left-hand escalator.

There was no panic at this stage because the fire was not producing much smoke, and indeed passengers were still using the other two escalators. Roger Bell met Colin Townsley, who went down the up-escalator furthest from the fire to take a closer look. Townsley told Bell they would need BA sets and they would 'make pumps four' – that is, call out two more crews. The scale of a fire is measured by the number of engines called, and there was no reason to believe that this was going to be more than a routine 'four-pump' fire, nothing at all to speak of.

Bell suggested to Townsley, 'You go up and take it from there, Guv, and I'll go down and stop the people from coming up.' As he went back up to the exit Townsley met another crew from Manchester Square Fire Station, which had arrived at exactly the same time as Bell's Clerkenwell crew. Townsley spoke to the Manchester Square station officer, Peter Osborne, and they agreed that they would need jets to put out the fire. In fact a Clerkenwell firefighter was already bringing a hose into the booking-hall area and waiting further orders. Three Manchester Square firefighter's went back to get their breathing apparatus. Three Clerkenwell firemen, waiting by the ticket office, now had their breathing apparatus on, but had not yet started it up. One of them approached Townsley, who told him: 'Go back and make pumps four – persons reported,' which is a warning in firefighter-speak that life could be in danger.

Although Sub-Officer Bell had by now stopped people from using the Piccadilly Line escalators, there were still people coming up into the concourse from the Victoria Line escalators and milling about. Leading Fireman David Flanagan had just turned to carry out Station Officer Townsley's orders and was walking to the ticket barrier when there was a sudden blast of heat and a great cloud of smoke, which instantly plunged the whole area into total darkness. Flanagan and two other firefighters had their BA sets on but had not had time to activate them. They ran for the exit in Pancras Road as the poisonous smoke and intense heat engulfed them. They could hear screaming and cries for help and as they staggered out into the fresh air they took with them people they came across who were still unaware that a lethal fire had exploded only yards away. The firefighters who had taken the hose into the booking hall had to drop it and run as well.

Outside, there was still no sign of the conflagration below as a second Soho crew arrived, two minutes after the first. Two minutes after that they saw thick smoke coming from the station and a crowd of people rushing from the subway entrance. Inside the concourse, Station Officer Townsley had been talking to Osborne, his counterpart from Manchester Square. They had heard a commotion at the head of the Victoria Line escalator. Osborne had gone to see what was going on when he heard a crash and looked round to see dense smoke and flames coming from the area at the top of the Piccadilly Line escalator that he had just left, only yards away. Flames licked the ceiling and flashed bright red before the smoke enveloped them in a moment.

Townsley was nowhere to be seen, but Osborne spotted another man emerging from the smoke, scorched by the heat, and took him down the Victoria Line escalator, at the same time trying to calm other passengers. At the bottom of the escalator Osborne doused the man with water and left a member of the public to continue soaking him while he

stopped any more passengers from going up to the concourse. The people below the fire were quite safe, and Roger Bell on the Piccadilly Line and Osborne on the Victoria Line waved the trains through. But nobody above ground had any idea what had happened to them: Bell had gone into the station without his radio.

What is so difficult to grasp about the King's Cross disaster is the timescale. When the fire exploded from the Piccadilly Line escalator into the booking hall, Townsley and the first crew had been at the station for between just three and four minutes. And while Bell and Osborne were marshalling passengers down on the platforms, thirty-one people, including Colin Townsley, died in the concourse and tunnels above them. When firefighters fought their way back in and found the bodies there was a clear pattern: nearly all of them were lying flat on their faces, having made a desperate dash to escape. But the super-heated fumes from the fire had caught them, collapsing their lungs and killing them almost instantly as they tried to flee. Some were subsequently burned by the flames themselves but in all cases the cause of death was probably asphyxiation.

Station Officer Townsley was not himself badly burned, although a woman lying near him, whom he might have been trying to rescue – the later inquiry certainly thought so – was. The fatal flash of the fire was over within seconds, and it was only after that that the business of fighting the blaze began. Roger Bell tried to tackle it from below with some makeshift equipment held by London Transport in an unmarked cupboard, but he had no idea what was going on above him, and there was little he could do.

The crews on the surface discussed ways of getting below the escalator fire as officers in ascending rank arrived on hearing the news that what had seemed an ordinary blaze had turned into a catastrophe. Station plans which the brigades should have had were hidden away behind some partitions screening work going on in the station. There were potential routes to the base of the fire, but they were not identified in time. Instead, the firefighters had the worst possible task: tackling the fire from above, inching towards it in black smoke

Firefighters at King's Cross had to fight the blaze from above, where it was hottest and the smoke thickest. Some got out just in time.

where the heat was most intense. The burning escalators, all of which had caught fire, were like a flaming chimney, the draughts of air from passing trains acting like a bellows at their base.

In the first few seconds of the battle, crews with breathing apparatus grabbed some badly burned casualties and dragged them out. Then the first men went in to tackle the blaze. All three staircases down to the

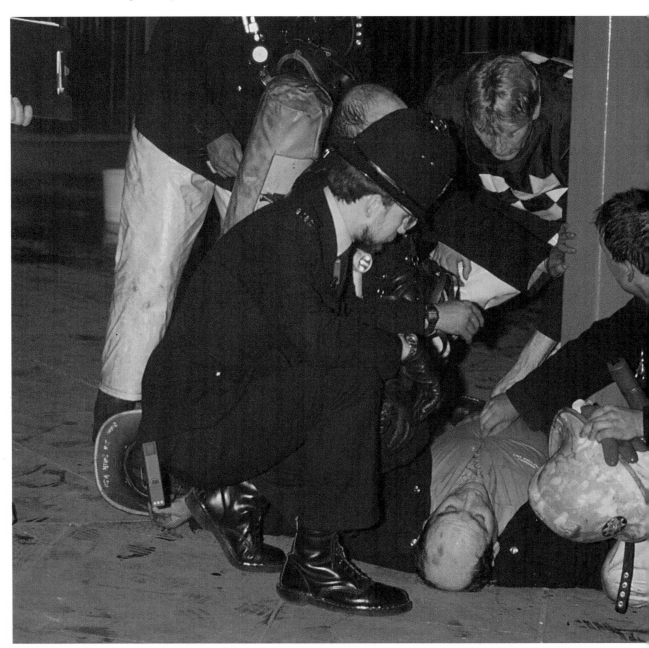

concourse below were used, the firefighters descending into the blackened and hellish inferno in relays, many stumbling out exhausted as the air-content warning whistles on their compressed-air apparatus sounded.

Among the first firefighters to go in was Steve Bell, a twenty-three-year-old who had arrived on the second Soho pump.

There was black smoke coming out of the Pancras Road entrance over the other side of the road. I thought: 'This is ugly.' I could hear screaming. We jumped over the barrier while the driver was getting the hose out and then we went down. We were pulling people out, but they were just falling down.

We moved into the tunnel [from the street to the booking hall] *and it was very, very hot. We had trouble with the nozzle which you usually use as a spray and which keeps some of the heat off. It was stuck on the jet. A few yards from the entrance something fell on us. It was this bloke, collapsed on us with his hair alight. Two guys grabbed him and pulled him out. We worked our way down the tunnel and it felt like miles, the heat hitting us in waves as the trains went through below. On the way down there was a set of stairs leading down to the concourse, and that is where we found the first body. It was in a right state, all shrivelled up.*

We worked our way along. It was incredibly hot. There's an old fireman's trick where you use your ears as

The intense heat of the King's Cross fire melted metal ticket machines in the ticket hall as a small fire on an escalator erupted into a fireball.

temperature gauges. Or you take off one of your gloves and put your hand up to tell which direction the heat is coming from. At King's Cross I tried it and the heat was coming from everywhere. On the right-hand side was the ticket office. It was shadowy, but all of a sudden the smoke would clear as a train went through, and then it was black again. I came to this metal thing – it must have been a ticket barrier – and I lifted the hose up and I felt myself being roasted. The jet was turning to steam. It was getting darker again and I started running out of air. I could hear the warning whistle on my breathing apparatus. I was spraying away and my mind was wandering and I was getting very tired. I started to forget how long my whistle had been going and I couldn't see how much air I had left.

David Priestman was in the same crew as Steve Bell. He remembers that nothing appeared to be happening when they first arrived – people were going in and out of the station as normal.

We heard a loud oomph and thick, black smoke poured out, together with screaming. I was the only one on the pump without a BA set allocated, but I ran down without any gear, holding my breath. Hordes of people were running past me. I was throwing people up the stairs to the entrance. There was a lot of yelling going on and I heard our leading firefighter shout: 'Get sets on, get sets on,' so I grabbed two people by their collars and dragged them up with me. I jumped over a fence and snatched the BA set allocated to the driver of the appliance. I dragged the hose down with the crew.

There was thick, black smoke to ground level and you couldn't see your hand. It was all by touch. The five of us started trying to make our way down to the ticket area. Right in front of us there was this guy on the floor. Most of his clothes had been burned off. I bent down

and picked him up and he felt as light as a feather – it must have been the adrenaline. The guy was taken out.

We tried to work our way to the ticket office and we were getting flash-overs going across the ceiling, really bright through the black smoke. Ceiling tiles were falling down alight. We were still in thick, black smoke; we could feel the heat, hear the screams. We were lying on our stomachs because of the heat. Balls of fire were going across all the time. We came to a gate that was actually pulled across and there was a pile of bodies there. People had tried to run out through the gate and that is where they died. This was only two to three minutes after the flash-over. We were the only crew down there at the time. Every time a train came through the station it was like a blast furnace. It was forcing air up the escalators giving the fire a nice, fresh blast and the ticket area would go bright orange. Virtually everything was alight, even metal.

Meanwhile, Steve Bell's colleague told him he had better get out as he was almost out of air.

As I was going back I heard a buckling and a huge bang. It was one of the ticket machines exploding. I saw a pink point of light. I went no more than ten yards before I smacked my head on a handrail. I thought there must be a body right there so I got out my torch and there it was. I started making my way out. I got to the entrance and the whistle on my BA set stopped, which meant I was out of air. I ripped the mask off. I was knackered. I looked up the stairs and thought, 'That's a long way up.' A couple of blokes from Westminster pulled me up and sat me down. There was steam coming off my shirt. A bloke from British Rail came up and threw a bucket of water over me.

David Priestman, too, got into trouble in the appalling conditions.

We were behind our jets – that was what was keeping us alive – and we were lying on the floor. At one stage I thought my ears had actually melted. Our gloves at the time had rubber in them, and they melted. I knew that if we shut that jet down we would fry.

We were down there for ten to fifteen minutes on our own. It was a very long time. I was getting very low on air – our BA should last three-quarters of an hour, but because of the extreme temperatures you were breathing harder. I was on the verge of collapsing and I suddenly felt this cold sensation on the back of my head. It was two firefighters with a hose reel cooling me down. My BA warning whistle started going. I staggered out by following the hose and collapsed. I then changed my cylinder and went back in. Crews were still turning up. It looked chaotic up there.

Using the hose as a guideline, Priestman went down into the station again and found that his colleague was suffering from delusions and did not know what he was doing. He got him out with the help of some other firefighters. 'By then I was absolutely knackered. My tunic was covered in fluids and fats from all the bodies – it was just grease all over. I hosed it down. We were all propped up against the fence, filthy and greasy.'

The battle to get the fire under control went on for nearly two hours, during which time many firefighters had narrow escapes when, in their fear and excitement, they waited until their warning whistles were sounding before staggering to the surface.

As the fire was fought and the news of its escalating seriousness went through to Central Control, London's deputy chief officer, Mike Doherty, who had been monitoring developments, set off for King's Cross. The fire was still burning when he got there, but it was under control and the men were beginning to put away their BA sets. Doherty took a look at the aftermath of this extraordinary blaze. The escalators and concourse, blackened and charred, were still strewn with badly burned bodies. 'Compared with some other conflagrations,' says Doherty, 'King's Cross was really a small fire, although it had such disastrous consequences.'

The blaze itself was generally described as a 'flash-over' – the sudden and simultaneous combustion of unburned gases at a critical heat, which creates a racing ball of fire, a rare, but by no means unknown, hazard for firefighters. Doherty does not believe that it was a flash-over so much as a rapid fire blown by draughts up a long section of escalator packed with years' worth of accumulated grease. One thing that struck him was that the wooden panels in the walls of the concourse were hardly charred at all. The heat had therefore been highly concentrated and funnelled. In fact two London Underground staff were released by firefighters from a toilet in the concourse when the blaze was under control. All it took to save them was a simple wooden door.

In pure firefighting terms, there was nothing very new at King's Cross. Doherty says:

The fire was put out with a hose – 95 per cent of fires are put out with water. Although the uniform is made of different material from when I joined the fire brigade in Essex in 1956, the firemen still wear a jacket and over-trousers. The hoses are plastic, and you don't have to hang them up to dry, but otherwise they are essentially the same, and we still get water from hydrants. The essence of the job is to get into the seat of the fire and cool it as soon as possible.

Whether or not the firemen who went to Smithfield with their old-fashioned oxygen breathing apparatus, nose pegs and goggles would have had a harder time tackling the King's Cross fire it is impossible to say. Most firefighters believe the outcome would not have been very different, except that the firefighters themselves might have taken more punishment. It is possible, too, that the intense heat might have turned the old pure oxygen cylinders of the BA sets into potential explosives. What has changed is the degree to

Many firefighters at King's Cross emerged exhausted, despite all the safety regulations in force to prevent them getting lost underground or running out of air.

which firefighters are safeguarded when they put on their BA sets and disappear into dense smoke in search of the fire. Their time is carefully logged with tags and a rescue crew is always standing by.

In the light of this, it might appear to the layman that Station Officer Townsley was foolhardy to have gone in with his men without breathing apparatus, and perhaps that he was not acting strictly according to the book. But in the first moments after his arrival his concern was to find out as fast as possible what was going on, what the danger was. Talking to his crew would have been difficult with the BA mask over his face. Had he and the other firemen who went into the station a

couple of minutes before the fire suddenly raged stopped to put on their BA sets, they might have arrived at the booking-hall concourse too late to prevent people from coming up the escalators, and the death toll could have been much higher. Colin Townsley himself was only a few yards away from safety when he died. He was incredibly unlucky, as firemen sometimes are.

The experience of Temporary Sub-Officer Roger Bell from Clerkenwell at the King's Cross fire underlines the point that there is nothing technology can do to change the fundamentally dangerous and unpredictable nature of firefighting. It was he who went down the escalator when Townsley went up. Bell was reported missing and many thought he must be dead, for he had no contact with the crews arriving above ground. In fact he was safe and sound below the fire, which he tackled, albeit unsuccessfully, with London Underground's makeshift hose.

It is perhaps surprising how little firefighters themselves feel that their job has changed between the Smithfield blaze of 1958 and the sudden and tragic fire at King's Cross in 1987. Yet no brilliant new method of putting out fires has been invented, and while

Station Officer Colin Townsley from Soho fire station died at King's Cross when he was caught in the blast along with passengers in the ticket hall.

the myriad smaller innovations which have made firefighting less dangerous are real enough, however high-tech your clothing, equipment and safety measures, it still takes guts to fight a fire.

It is a truism among firefighters that they are the only rescue workers who rush into a danger zone when others are rushing out. But there is one other aspect of their work which, though much less common, can be even more dangerous than firefighting. From time to time a building is reduced to rubble by a gas explosion or a bomb, and beneath the rubble an unknown number of people is trapped. It is primarily the firefighter's job to find the victims and dig them out – at the same time taking care not to kill themselves in the search.

CHAPTER FIVE
THE CALL FOR SILENCE

In April 1938, while still seeking peace with Hitler, the British government began to create defences on the home front. Local councils appointed their first honorary air raid precaution officers (ARPs) and started to recruit volunteers for the civil defence force. This was to be a civilian emergency service, trained to defend the country against invasion and to go to the rescue if war broke out and bombs began to fall.

London was thought to be especially vulnerable, and it was assumed that in the first air raids the death toll would be massive – perhaps 250,000 within a few days.

The government took the view that it was up to local authorities to get themselves organized for the anticipated Armageddon, and there were many arguments about whether the defence of the nation was the

Searching for survivors in the rubble of a building bombed during the Blitz: this work was done by the light and heavy rescue services of civil defence.

responsibility of the town halls or Whitehall. It was a characteristic episode in the history of emergency services in Britain: the nation was faced with the prospect of an aerial bombardment equivalent to a succession of earthquakes, volcanic eruptions and hurricanes which would smash to pieces the largely Victorian fabric of its inner cities, yet the government appeared to be satisfied that a bit of unpaid voluntary effort would suffice to pick up the pieces.

Nevertheless it was self-evident that the existing fire, ambulance, police and medical services could not possibly cope with the scale of destruction expected in air raids. And there would be a need for a kind of rescue work which in peacetime was very rare: the search for casualties buried dead or alive in the rubble of collapsed buildings. Anyone might lend a hand shifting the debris, but it was recognized that a specialist service might be required to control this work. The locally-run rescue service of the wartime civil defence came into being.

During the years of the Blitz, these civil defence rescue teams developed, in cities throughout Britain, an understanding of what the emergency services would today call 'collapsed-structure' rescue. In time their experience became invaluable to other countries throughout the world. When the war ended in 1945, a reformed civil defence continued to train recruits to handle bombing raids, which, happily, never came. Twenty years later, the civil defence volunteers were effectively disbanded; and since 1945 the job of rescuing people from collapsed buildings has been taken over by the fire service who have no special training for or developed expertise in dealing with this kind of rescue work, although it could be of vital importance in the future. The problem is a classic one for the emergency services: they need such skills, but there are not enough incidents to justify training, as there were in the last war.

With so many young men in the forces, the wartime civil defence rescue teams tended to be made up of recruits too old to fight, but vigorous and knowledgeable enough to tackle the dangerous and delicate task of digging people out of the shattered timbers and broken brickwork of bombed buildings. When war broke out in September 1939, these rescue services were established, usually under the building works departments of local councils, with recruits from private building firms. They were small teams of between eight and ten men with a knowledge of building structures, based at depots from which they could be called when the bombs began to fall. Their expertise was enshrined in a series of civil defence manuals, illustrated with black and white photographs, which set out step by step how to go about the task of extricating live casualties from demolished buildings.

Volunteers were divided into 'light rescue' and 'heavy rescue' services. The first category consisted mainly of stretcher-bearers, who cared for the walking wounded and surface casualties. The heavy rescue teams searched for people buried deep in the rubble; it was these which took on the most difficult jobs – entire terraces demolished, hospitals and schools reduced to rubble, with live casualties possibly buried deep beneath the debris.

In *The War Over Walthamstow*, his 1945 account of civil defence in the London borough of Walthamstow (which was then part of Essex) Ross Wyld pays tribute to the work of these men.

The heavy rescue men, from their practical experience of the construction of buildings, had a knowledge which was exceedingly valuable and, in many cases of serious difficulty, rescue work was effected without loss of life simply because of the knowledge which these men had of the possibilities as well as the dangers of dealing with wrecked buildings.

One of the most interesting and heart-warming experiences at an incident was to see the faces of the men after they had rescued a trapped casualty from a particularly difficult situation. They would work for hours under the most gruelling conditions, would refuse to be relieved by other squads and then, at the end of their labours, be more than rewarded by the extrication alive of a man or woman or child who had been buried for some hours.

It will be appropriate to record here that eighty-four men, 101 women, and thirty-four children were rescued in Walthamstow from debris wherein they had been trapped, and although light rescue and wardens made some of the rescues the bulk of these people owed their rescue to the heavy rescue service. In addition, five horses were rescued from stables . . . Apart from rescue of human beings, dogs, cats, chickens, ducks, rabbits, canaries, parakeets and even tame mice came within the ambit of the rescue service, and many an owner had reason to bless the men for restoring a prized pet.

It was the civil defence heavy rescue teams, like this one in action in Walthamstow during the Second World War, that developed an expertise in finding survivors in bombed buildings.

Typically, as in the evolution of all emergency services, the expertise of these rescue teams was hard won through experience, and it was essentially eminently practical and founded in common sense. There were bad ways of searching the rubble of demolished buildings, and good ways, as advocated by the civil defence manuals. They had no sophisticated equipment, but made do with what was at hand, tunnelling into bombed buildings using broken joists and splintered timbers as props. Of the heavy-rescue gear available in Walthamstow, Wyld says: 'The equipment . . . was augmented from time to time until the heavy van or lorry which was required . . . resembled in some respects a Christmas tree, for it carried not only picks and shovels but ladders, crowbars, debris baskets, and so on.'

Heavy rescue teams had little technology: what they developed was technique. If they were to find casualties buried alive they had to guess where they might be. Information from survivors and neighbours was invaluable. If they knew the layout of a building, they could work out in which part of it the victims were likely to have been at the time the bomb was dropped. Then they looked at how the collapse had happened, and guessed whether walls might have fallen inwards in such a way as to provide protective cavities. And once the surface casualties had been found in the thick dust and debris the teams would call for silence among the rescue workers and those gathered anxiously around the bomb site. Someone would shout: 'Is there anybody there?' and everyone would listen intently. If there was a reply, those who heard it would point to provide a 'fix' on the likely location of the trapped person. This procedure would be repeated as they gingerly removed rubble, taking care not to cause any further collapse. Sometimes they would decide to tunnel into the debris, calling all the time as they homed in on the buried victim. And then the call for silence would be repeated as they got further and further in, until there were no replies and their hope was gone. Then only bodies would be recovered from the rubble.

During the Blitz there were some remarkable rescues, though very few of them have been recorded. This kind of search was so commonplace at the time as to be hardly worth a mention in dispatches. But one or two were unusual enough to attract medical attention. In the *British Medical Journal* of 19 April 1945, a Dr G. S. Swann records the following incident, without revealing where it happened (doubtless for security reasons).

On a Thursday at 1am a bomb struck a block of three-storey cellared houses. Some of these houses were completely destroyed. As it was known that a number of people were in them at the time of the disaster, rescue work started almost at once, but with little hope of saving anyone alive. At 6pm on Friday, an elderly woman was rescued alive, but in such serious condition that she died a few days later.

At 7pm on Sunday I was sent for as the rescue squad had heard a voice under the debris. On arrival I made contact with the trapped girl, one of my own patients,

Miss F. B., aged twenty-one, whose voice could faintly be heard, obviously at some distance below the debris. She told me her name, that she knew her father and mother were dead, and that she was quite immobile except for a little movement of the left hand. It was astonishing to find her completely intelligent, and throughout the six hours before she was finally removed, at 1am on Monday – exactly ninety-six hours from the time she was first trapped – she retained her intelligence and was of great help in guiding the rescue squad in their difficult task.

At 9.30pm, debris having been removed entirely by hand and several wooden beams sawn through, a narrow hole four feet in depth allowed contact with the girl's left hand. It was just possible to feel her pulse, which was well perceptible at about ninety beats per minute.

A short time afterwards her head was uncovered, when it became obvious she was face downwards in position. By means of a length of rubber tubing and a feeding cup we succeeded in getting her to rinse out her mouth, after which she was allowed to swallow a little hot, well-sugared tea. Shortly afterwards, as more of her body became exposed, I gave her one-third of a grain of morphine, and about quarter-hourly sips of tea, by now out of the feeding cup direct. By midnight she was completely exposed at the bottom of a deepish hole. The rescue squad also succeeded in burrowing sideways at her body level, a burrow sufficient to admit head and shoulders with debris supported by some flooring crossbeams. It was through this burrow that we succeeded in delivering her.

She was lying, crouched face down, her knees on her chest and heels under her buttocks, her right arm under her chest and left arm by the side of her face – a normal breech position. Across her back was the dead body of her father. It was evident we dared not remove him before the girl, so we arranged the rescue squad with one man from above easing the dead body as much as possible, another down the main hold supporting the chin, and a third grasping her hips and gently pulling her through the small narrow side burrow. As she was being removed she told us there was a woman alive next door. Once on the warm stretcher I immediately straightened her legs and sent her to hospital.

This was a classic example of wartime rescue work involving a variety of techniques, including tunnelling, to free someone whose exact position and condition was unknown until hours after the excavation began. It was unusual only in the fact that this girl had actually survived in such a cramped position without food or water for four days. Her father, who was lying on top of her, had stayed alive for two days and both victims could hear the rescue workers above them, but such was the density of rubble that their own feeble calls for help were not picked up. Only when layers of bricks and timber had been removed did the voice of the girl break through.

When she told them there was someone alive next door whose calls she had heard, a second rescue began. This is Dr Swann's account of it.

After shouting we heard a voice say, 'I am A.D. – I am all right, and walking about in the cellar. I have a baby with me, who is not very well, and we have some bottles of milk.' This turned out to be delirium, and it was some hours before contact was made. It was then discovered that she was lying on the cellar stairs, her head higher than her feet, and completely immobile.

The only way to deliver her was through a narrow aperture formed by the absence of the upper panel of a door, the rest of the door supporting a mass of debris. It was impossible to risk cutting away the side of the door, but it was possible to remove a triangular piece of the lower panel. Her pulse was weaker than the girl's but countable at about 100. She also received morphine, and was fed in a similar way to the first patient. The dead body of a three-and-a-half-year-old boy was lying under her right arm. To deliver her through this narrow aperture one man was able to see inside the hole and just scramble down to place both hands under her shoulders; another man, lying on the debris, held by his heels, was just able to reach her legs. I lay over the aperture and, as she was eased upwards, succeeded in grasping her shoulders and bringing her out of the hole over my own right shoulder to stretcher-bearers behind. This was at 6am on the Monday, 101 hours after she was buried.

This second woman, who was thirty-four years old, thought her little boy had lived for nearly three days after the bomb had buried them. And she too said she had been able to hear the rescue workers above her even though she and her child were not found for so long.

Dr Swann's report was written thirteen days after the rescue, when both women were recovering well from their injuries, shock, dehydration and lack of food. The lesson, the doctor felt, was that it should always be assumed in rescue work that there might be survivors, and he recommended that local-authority rescue teams should acquire some sound detectors to make it easier to hear the faint cries of people buried very deeply.

What kind of sound detectors Dr Swann had in mind at that time we do not know, for it was a long time before listening devices designed to detect people buried in rubble were brought into use in Britain. However good the rubble-search techniques of the wartime heavy rescue teams, they must all have longed for some new kind of technology which would penetrate the debris and provide a more accurate means of locating survivors than calling and listening. But no such technology was available during the Blitz, nor in the last year of the war when new weapons began to rain down on London: the V1 rockets, or pilotless planes, and the V2 missiles which caused greater destruction than the bombs of the Blitz. The V1s were those terrifying short-winged rockets known as doodlebugs or buzzbombs because their engines could be heard above by those scurrying for their basements and shelters, who listened intently for the noise to stop as the engines cut. There were usually three or four seconds of silence as the doodlebug fell to earth, and then the explosion. The V2s made no sound at all until they exploded.

The first of the doodlebugs landed on London on 13 June 1944, and the first of the V2s in September. These attacks continued until just before the end of the war. The doodlebugs killed more than 6,000 and the V2s nearly 3,000 people, mostly Londoners.

Once again the heavy rescue squads went to work digging people from the rubble. And the fire brigade became more involved in these searches because, devastating though their effects were, these rockets carried no incendiary devices and there were therefore fewer fires to be put out than there had been in the Blitz. From the many small local-authority fire services that existed before the war, a national fire service had been created after the Blitz, and it was operational when the rocket attacks came.

Cyril de Marne was in the fire service in West Ham, a district of London's heavily bombed East End, throughout the war. Whereas in the Blitz he had done very little rescue work, it was different with the doodlebugs. He recalls:

We had advanced intelligence about these rockets and we knew they would not have incendiary devices, so we were reorganized so that the firemen became more involved in searching for people in bombed buildings. I was fairly senior by then, and I remember taking training courses from the civil defence heavy rescue teams. We got involved in a lot of this kind of work.

When we turned up we would ask the wardens who knew the street which had been hit where the front doors were so that we could get an idea of the layout of rooms and where people might be. We would rescue first the people who were on the surface or only lightly trapped. Then the leader of the rescue team would shout, 'Quiet, quiet,' and we would listen for any sounds or voices. We found quite a few people in that way.

And the RAF would turn up with their dogs and ask where there might be people buried. They would let the dogs go, and at first they would just seem to go all over the place without any direction, but then they would stop and start digging. We found many people like this, alive as well as dead. The dogs never seemed to fail.

It was after one of the worst of the V2 rocket attacks on Walthamstow, in December 1944, that Ross Wyld recalls the first use of rescue dogs, which, he says in his local history of civil defence, 'from time to time proved very useful in indicating casualties hidden below debris, although they were not by any means infallible'.

Wyld says that the official policy when a V2 rocket landed was to pretend something else had caused the explosion so that 'no indication was given to the enemy of the arrival of these missiles'. Local authorities were advised by the London region headquarters to announce that blasts were 'those of gas mains, ammunition wagons or delayed-action bombs'.

These last attacks of the V2 rockets were, in fact, more akin to the sudden and unexpected explosions that continued to occur in peacetime because, as the weapons travelled faster than sound, they could not be heard. No sirens sounded to warn people to get into shelters as they had in the Blitz; there was not even the few seconds' grace to rush for cover afforded by the noise of the buzzbomb's engine above the rooftops.

When the war was over, the civil defence

heavy rescue teams were not disbanded entirely. Instead they were re-established to form part of a volunteer force retained under Home Office control in the event of war breaking out again. After the bombing of Hiroshima and Nagasaki in August 1945, and the terrifying news that Russia had nuclear weapons, there was a very real fear that Britain might soon face a holocaust far worse than the Blitz. So the civil defence corps continued to train and to carry out exercises in which it rehearsed for the massive rescue operation that would follow a nuclear attack. Its manuals, drawing largely on wartime experience, were constantly updated.

But these civil defence volunteers had no peacetime function. Instead the job of freeing people when from time to time a gas explosion wrecked a building or shopping centre was handed over to the fire brigades, which after 1946, reverted to the control of the local authorities. Some of the contemporary firemen, like Cyril de Marne, had already been trained in this kind of rescue at the end of the war, but new recruits were not. Whereas the civil defence volunteers had many training grounds around the country, the need for collapsed-structure rescue was so rare that the fire services understandably felt specific training for their own personnel in such techniques would be uneconomic.

This is, by and large, still the case – even though the fire brigade has taken on the responsibility for rubble searches when a building collapses. Since the old civil defence corps training grounds disappeared in 1968, when Prime Minister Harold Wilson withdrew nearly all of their budget, there has been no centre of expertise in collapsed-structure rescue in Britain. While the Fire Service College at Moreton-in-Marsh has mock-up motorway pile-ups and smashed trains on which fire officers can practise and learn the skills of extrication, there are no facilities simulating the conditions involved in searching amid the rubble of demolished buildings. In 1987, a Home Office working party did suggest that extra money should be provided to set up courses at Moreton so that some training in collapsed-structure rescue would be available if war threatened again, and to improve peacetime knowledge, but nothing was done. Nor does this type of rescue work figure much in the Manuals of Firemanship.

There have been very few peacetime explosions devastating enough to make the headlines. But for the people of Glasgow, there is one disaster which lives in the memory. It happened in the quiet suburb of Clarkston on the afternoon of 21 October 1971, when a gas explosion with the force of a V2 rocket killed and injured in one horrific blast more people than many of the enemy's ballistic missiles in the last war.

A gas leak had been reported in the local shopping centre, a single-storey block with a car park on top and a basement area below. When PC Dave Hill, of what was then the Renfrew and Bute Constabulary, passed the shopping centre slowly in his patrol car at around 3pm, he saw gas board men at work.

They were drilling holes in the road – I don't know why. I had just passed them and was about fifty yards away in the car when I heard not a bang, but a kind of 'fullumph' and saw flames shooting halfway across the road. I sat there for a couple of seconds and I just couldn't take it in; it was very hard to believe something like this had happened. I ran to a local garage and dialled 999, and then went back to look for casualties. The shops had collapsed, the car park on top had come down, and the whole lot had fallen into the basement.

The gas board man I had seen was dead. A girl who had been getting off a bus parked opposite had been decapitated. I started digging in the rubble with my bare hands and was finding bodies. I don't remember getting anybody out alive. When I went round to the back of the shopping centre, the whole wall had been blown out. There

was a woman standing there who had been trying a dress on in a changing room. She was only half dressed but she was uninjured. Later the fire brigade called for silence and we listened, but I don't remember hearing any calls – everybody had either been rescued or was already dead. We had had exercises before because we were near Glasgow Airport and there were emergency plans for a plane coming down, but we never expected a disaster on this scale.

A gas explosion in 1971 demolished this two-storey shopping centre in the Glasgow suburb of Clarkston, leaving 20 people dead.

Another policeman, Ian Gardiner, heard on his radio that there had been an explosion and was there minutes later.

It was, oh my God, some surprise when I got there. I ran straight across and met David, and we heard wailing and screaming coming from the shopping centre. Some people were just lying there; others were buried up to their necks in concrete, some of them alive, some of them dead. We were tunnelling into the concrete with our hands. Mine were all cut, and I got enamel in my eyes from the tiles which had melted. There were clouds of dust and you couldn't tell who were the policemen, they were so covered in dust.

Sub-officer Andrew Bell was in charge of the first fire crew to arrive. He remembers:

It was horrendous, like a battlefield. The cars on the car park were hanging at an angle and there was a double-decker bus with its windows blown out and people underneath it. There was some fire, but it was from gas so we couldn't put it out. All the same, we ran out some hose and just got stuck in. At one point we realized we were standing on dead bodies under the rubble in the road. I had only become a sub-officer the year before, and it was the first time I had seen anything on this scale, and in my thirty years in the fire service it is still easily the worst thing I attended.

We put some ladders across the basement and got in and got some people out alive, but there were also people there who did not look as if they had been touched, yet they were dead. I was in the basement when we heard the calls for silence and we stood and listened but we did not hear anybody. That was repeated several times.

The heavy concrete structure of the building made rescue work especially difficult, and the fire brigade then had very little equipment to cut through it or move it. 'It all had to be done by hand,' Andrew Bell recalls. The final death

toll at Clarkston was twenty, making it one of the worst disasters in postwar history, and many were injured.

The rescue operation itself, which involved hundreds of people picking over the rubble, was certainly no more sophisticated than anything done by the civil defence volunteers during the war. In fact, it is arguable that it was less sophisticated. By 1971, few firemen with any wartime experience remained in the service and the peacetime civil defence teams who might have trained the newer firefighters

Nobody was found alive beneath the concrete slabs at Clarkston, although there were regular 'calls for silence' in the hope of hearing cries for help.

had disappeared along with all their training grounds in 1968. When a catastrophe like that at Clarkston happened the firefighters simply had to draw on their general knowledge of buildings and unsafe structures, learned in firefighting training, and their ability to turn their hand to any kind of problem.

Looking back, Andrew Bell feels that the whole operation would have been handled differently today. 'Now we've got so much equipment that we can call on specialist rescue appliances with cutting gear, lifting gear and obviously things like the thermal-imaging camera.'

Even those wartime firemen who maintain that some of the expertise in rescue technique might have been lost when the civil defence squads went out of action after the war, believe that modern technology provides wonderful new ways of searching for casualties. 'Things have moved on with these infrared cameras and so on,' says Cyril de Marne. New electronic devices which appear to fulfil the wartime dreams of Dr Swann of detection equipment which could swiftly pinpoint survivors in the rubble of a collapsed building do exist, and are owned now by many fire services around Britain. Yet the idea that they have made much difference to collapsed-structure rescue is largely a myth. Because building collapses are so unusual in Britain, few firefighters ever get a chance to put them to a practical test. Those who have had to go to the rescue without them can only imagine how valuable they would have been, while those who have had them to hand generally dismiss them as a waste of time.

Just before the new technology became generally available, one of the most spectacular explosions since the war shattered windows, tore the heads off parking meters and hurled debris into the sea in Brighton, Sussex. Whereas the Clarkston explosion had demolished a postwar building of giant concrete slabs, the Brighton bomb, as it turned out to be, took a huge chunk out of the Grand Hotel, a stuccoed Victorian building of brick and timber on the seafront, with old-fashioned plumbing. This blast really was reminiscent of the Blitz, and although the firefighters of the East Sussex Fire Brigade who went to the rescue were too young to remember it themselves, they faced the same kind of search as those heavy rescue teams of the old civil defence.

The explosion happened in the early hours of 12 October 1984, the fourth day of the Conservative Party Conference, which was being held at the Grand Hotel. Some of the party leaders had already gone to bed, others were still up socializing, and the prime minister, Margaret Thatcher, working late as always, was reading through a document in her suite before turning in.

Despite the police security at the hotel, an IRA terrorist had managed to plant a bomb in Room 629, at the top of the building, right above Margaret Thatcher's room. It had been set by microchip to detonate at 3am. It actually went off at 2.54am, wrecking the rooms immediately adjacent and toppling a huge Victorian chimney stack, which crashed through the century-old fabric of the building, taking with it a huge pile of rubble in which sleeping delegates were buried.

From the seafront it looked as if a great slab had been taken out of the upper floors of the building, which were now open to the sea breezes, but inside the central core of one section of the building was piled up between the basement and the ground floor.

Mrs Thatcher herself narrowly avoided this assassination attempt because she had not gone to bed earlier, and many other bloodied and dust-covered survivors had miraculous escapes. Only five of those in the hotel died, four before any rescuers could reach them and one later in hospital. Yet the task of the firefighters who searched the rubble for survivors was one of the most difficult and painstaking in postwar history. They were no better equipped for this work than the civil defence rescue teams of forty years earlier, and for nearly every one of them, if not all, it was an entirely new challenge.

Firefighters at the Grand Hotel, Brighton, which was bombed in 1984, used all their ingenuity and any equipment they could find to search for survivors in the rubble.

It was the job of the police to take a roll call, to find out as much as they could about who might have been in the collapsed part of the Grand Hotel when the bomb exploded. They knew that there were 220 registered guests and eleven staff on duty, but there had been various parties and meetings in the hotel earlier and some non-residents attending might still have been in the building, so the list of potential casualties was unknown.

In collapsed-structure rescue, the first and most difficult task is guessing who might have been in a building, where exactly they are likely to have been, and how many people could potentially be in the rubble. While the first searches began, the police drew up their lists, checking and cross-checking the whereabouts of guests and possible visitors to the Grand Hotel.

Fire crews headed towards the hotel from all over Sussex. With the firefighters from Hove were Leading Fireman Ken Towner and his sub-officer, Colin Finlay. Towner went up an old fire escape at the back of the building to the fifth floor. He looked out towards what had been the front of the hotel and there was the sea. Water was dripping from a severed pipe on to the remains of the hotel rooms. Embedded in the rubble on the precipitous edge of the demolished façade was the giant frame of Harvey Thomas, 6ft 4ins tall and weighing 18 stone. He was buried up to his neck and unable to move, his legs facing seaward. Fireman Mick Ayling heard his calls and he and Ken Towner worked their way gingerly towards him. A delegate to the conference, surgeon David Skidmore, who had heard the explosion and dashed to the hotel from his lodgings wearing his jogging gear, joined them. Ken remembers:

The alarm bells were ringing and water was cascading down. Mick Ayling went forward when he heard Harvey Thomas's voice, and I think we put a blanket around him. But we did not have a clue how to get him out. We started moving the debris but Mick cut himself and had to go back. I took over and gradually we got him free. We got an Epco, a device used for pushing out panels in cars which we had for extricating people in road accidents, and eased the pressure on him. I just told him to push with his leg, and that I'd pull, and he came out like a cork out of a bottle.

Thomas, whose wife was back home in Finchey, heavily pregnant with their first child, was the conference co-ordinator. He had been in the room above the one in which the bomb had exploded and had been blown to the ceiling before falling two floors and

becoming trapped 60ft above ground. The firefighters who freed him had to wear safety ropes as they pulled the debris clear.

Of the other rescues from the upper floors, the most difficult began when firefighters heard voices in an area roughly level with the roof of the foyer, where a tangle of broken beams, mangled bedsteads and other debris hung precariously, having fallen in a great pile of dust from several floors above.

Norman Tebbit, Trade and Industry Secretary, and his wife Margaret were entombed in this mass. Slowly and cautiously, firefighters cut through to them. It took until 7am to get them out, Margaret, who was seriously injured, first; the minister a little later. He had been saved from more damaging injuries by the fact that he had stayed with the bed as he tumbled down, whereas his wife had fallen out.

There were repeated calls for silence in the rescue operation, and in the debris above the Tebbits a voice was heard faintly. 'What is your name?' a fireman asked. The reply came: 'John W. A. K. E. H. A. M.' The surname spelled out was that of the Tory Chief Whip. The firefighters knew where he was, but the problem was getting him out without causing the debris to collapse.

Colin Finlay, the sub-officer from Hove, took on the task of releasing him. Colin and two others had to tunnel into the rubble to get to him.

We were on a high having got the Tebbits out, but this was new ground for us. We had never done any tunnelling before. We had to have a strategy. John Wakeham was under 12ft of rubble and we could not go in from the top in case it all came down. We were using chainsaws to cut the big timbers – and I had never used these before – and bolt-cutters to get through the mattresses, but the most useful tools were our hands. From a local hire shop we got Acrow props to shore up the tunnel and eventually we got to a tuft of hair which was John Wakeham's. We finally had to use a wedgie, the older

The scene of the bombed Victorian Grand Hotel in Brighton: a huge chimney stack toppled over and crashed down through the building.

spreading equipment we had for road-accident extrication, to get him out of the last bit. He was very lucid throughout, and a big cheer went up when we got him out.

It was not until around 10.30am that John Wakeham was released. Tragically, his wife was one of the five people who were killed by the bomb.

Looking back on this remarkable piece of rescue work ten years on, the firefighters involved do not all agree on whether or not the equipment they have now would have made much difference to their approach or methods. Colin Finlay, now an assistant divisional officer, believes thermal-imaging cameras and the new heavy rescue gear the fire-brigade tenders carry would have made the job easier. But Bob Stevenson, assistant chief fire officer of the East Sussex Brigade at the time, and now retired, disagrees.

There is no 'quick fix' for this kind of rescue. It is really no different from the civil defence heavy rescue squads after a V2 rocket attack. It's manual labour, hard manual labour, and command and control, and doing what is humanly possible. We did have the army in with infrared cameras, but there were hot-water pipes and heating in the basement, so thermal-imaging cameras would have made no difference. Acoustic listening devices might have been useful, but thermal-imaging cameras, which are brilliant for training firemen in thick smoke, are no good for this kind of search because they cannot see through solid objects. Maybe in a building made of big concrete slabs heavy lifting gear might have been useful, but the Grand Hotel was a traditional building and you could not use any heavy machinery on it.

Not long before the Grand Hotel bombing, the London Fire Brigade had been experimenting with thermal-imaging cameras as an aid to firefighting. Excitement in the press and interest from fire brigades, both in Britain and abroad, about this new equipment was stirred about three months after that disaster when, on a cold January morning in 1985, an opportunity arose to test its effectiveness in detecting bodies in a demolished building.

People living in a block of flats, Newnham House, in Putney, south London had been complaining about a gas leak, but the source of it had not been found. On the morning of Thursday 10 January, a fifteen-year-old paperboy, Ian Connor, arrived at Newnham House and almost became a victim of an explosion which wrecked the block with one gigantic blast. 'I was thrown from my feet by an almighty bang,' he was quoted as saying at the time. 'There was a big blue flash of light. The flats simply crumbled down; glass and smashed trees flew everywhere. I was thrown against a wall and suffered concussion.'

Again, the rubble of the building was reminiscent of the bomb damage of wartime Britain, and the emergency services arrived to pick up the pieces. Inquiries were made about who might have been in the building, and the area – soon surrounded by crowds – was cordoned off. The firefighters went to work to look for survivors. They made one remarkable rescue when, after more than three hours of searching, they heard a faint tapping sound. There were the customary calls for silence and the tapping was heard again. Excavation of the rubble began from two directions, above and below.

The old civil defence manuals, founded on wartime experience, explained that live casualties were usually found in small cavities where a wall had toppled sideways and its fall had been checked by some other object. This was the case once again at Newnham House, where a thirty-five-year-old Czech-born woman, Eve Kretjci, had been in the bathroom of her flat when the explosion occurred. Her sister, in the same flat, had been killed, along with seven residents of other flats. But Miss Kretjci was saved by chance when she was trapped in a tent-like hollow of rubble. It was only when the debris above her had been painstakingly removed by rescue workers that she could be heard tapping on the side of the bath.

Firefighter Peter Simpson recounts the story of the rescue.

I came on duty at 9am. I was based at Lewisham, riding in charge of the emergency rescue tender, and we came on as relief for the first crews at about 9.30am, by which time a lot of searching had already been done.

As my crew continued the search, one of my colleagues came across a foot hidden in the rubble and we began excavating. A doctor was able to tell us it was a female foot, and it was in that area that we heard a faint knocking sound at about 10am.

An assistant divisional officer called for silence and we could hear the faint tapping again. We began to excavate from two directions to where there was a sort of void in the rubble. My crew and myself tunnelled in, shoring up with bits of wood, until we had gone about eight to ten feet. We eventually came to Eve Kretjci. The floor section had collapsed from above, leaving a small area which protected her, like a triangle.

She had a really bad leg injury, and was covered in debris and trapped by a towel rail and other things that had fallen

A gas explosion demolished Newnham House, Putney, in the winter of 1985. Nobody knew how many people might be buried in the rubble when the search began.

When, after some time, a faint cry for help was heard in the rubble at Putney, firefighters began to find a way to the trapped woman.

on her. We came at her feet first from a narrow tunnel, and we thought the other crew coming from the other side would get to her first, but they couldn't get through.

They called for a relief to take over, but when you are doing something like that you get involved – it is a bit like 'pick-a-sticks', and once you have worked on the tunnel from the start you know every detail of it – so we said we *would prefer to carry on. There were four or five of us working there.*

When we first began to break through I was at the head of the tunnel and was able to make contact with Miss Kretjci by reaching out with my hand and touching her. That's when we called the doctor in. We were going to have to bring her out feet first, and because her leg was badly hurt, held together by only a few sinews, we could not turn her round or get a stretcher down, so bringing her out that way would mean putting pressure on her legs. The problem was whether we should spend more time excavating around her to bring her out intact, or whether she would die if we did not get her out more quickly. The doctor went down and decided she had to come out. She remembers hearing firemen talking about cutting off her leg, but we never considered that.

So Eve Kretjci was eased out and, though badly injured, lived to tell the tale. Her excavation was achieved in classic fashion with absolutely no use of any new technology at all, and it was the first and last time Peter Simpson had to tackle such a difficult rescue operation. It was dangerous for all his crew because of the instability of the rubble, but he explains: 'You don't think about the danger at the time, because you become very involved, and you are used to working as a team and trusting other people around you. You rely on them.'

Peter had no training in this kind of rescue but he believes that firefighters have a good all-round knowledge of how to tackle a variety of problems.

In London, on the emergency rescue tender course you do training for rescue in a sewer collapse, which is similar, with, maybe, a small sewer stuffed full of debris. They let you as a crew get on with it. We are seen as the jacks-of-all-trades, and we have to do some unusual things – it's part of the job. You apply your judgement and tackle a specific situation as best you can.

While Peter Simpson and his crew were carefully releasing Eve Kretjci, the attention of the press was attracted by the activity of other firefighters, who were scanning the disaster site with a new-fangled piece of equipment: thermal-imaging cameras. Although Miss Kretjci was the only survivor of the building collapse, this was not known until some hours afterwards, and it was claimed in the press that the cameras had at least helped to find the dead in the rubble – eight people had lost their lives. As the search continued and debris was carefully sifted and removed, it appeared that the cameras, described by one newspaper as 'incredibly sophisticated', had ushered in a whole new era in rescue techniques. One report maintained that orders were flooding in for the new camera from other fire brigades and police forces.

However, this new piece of equipment was

The one survivor of the Putney gas explosion is brought out on a stretcher.

not viewed as such a revolutionary development by some members of the fire brigade. Peter Simpson recalls:

The thermal-imaging camera was featured in the Tomorrow's World *television programme, and friends of mine said how fantastic it was. It was heralded as the great X-ray vision thing, but all firefighters know that it is no good for this kind of search. I have done exercises with them myself showing that if you put a man on one side of a piece of*

---

glass, the camera cannot pick up his image on the other.

The thermal-imaging camera said to have been used to find the woman trapped in the Putney explosion. In fact it is virtually useless for this kind of search and is only used by fire brigades for seeing through smoke.

The infrared or thermal-imaging camera has a long history. It was first of interest to the military because of its ability to 'see' in the dark. But it reacts to heat rather than light, and displays an image which reflects a temperature range. Out in the open it can easily pick up body heat, but it cannot 'see through' solid objects – not even glass – if the heat source is not sufficient to penetrate them itself.

A live person in rubble will emit heat, but

at a low level, and a dead body will emit none at all unless some is generated by decomposition. If in a rubble search there is a gap, a clear airway, through to part of a body, the thermal-imaging camera could pick that up. But in a collapsed building there are also all kinds of other heat sources: cookers in use when an explosion occurred which have not yet cooled down; hot-water pipes; materials heated by fires. So if a camera registers heat, it does not necessarily mean it has found a body – in fact, if a heat source is misinterpreted, it can easily send a rescue party on a fruitless search. There are some special circumstances in which the thermal-imaging camera could be helpful – in a darkened basement, for example, where a body might be slumped on the floor – but it would be no good at all at finding someone buried in as much debris as John Wakeham was in Brighton.

A report by the Fire and Research Department of the Home Office in 1992 surveyed the detection devices acquired by fire brigades at that time, and asked for assessments of their effectiveness. Two thirds of brigades, forty-four in all, had access to thermal-imaging cameras, either as part of their emergency-rescue equipment or available on special request. Not surprisingly, the cameras had not been used very often to search for people in collapsed buildings because of the infrequency of such calamities. Although twenty-five brigades had used them, they had done so on average only five times in a single year. And they were not thought to be of much value. The report summary reads:

Thermal-imaging cameras are of limited use for locating hidden or buried casualties in a building-collapse situation. Their limitation is that some part of the body must be visible to the naked eye, or, if hidden, in contact with a thin obscuring material such as a partition, for the camera to be able to detect its presence.

The display of standard cameras is limited to shades of grey to depict different temperatures. This means that unless the operator is very skilled, it is difficult to give an accurate interpretation of temperature, and it is also very difficult to detect small changes in temperature over time.

These cameras are very useful for finding hot spots during firefighting and for locating the seat of fires in situations where it may be hidden or obscured. However, their use for detecting buried casualties during building collapse is minimal, to the point of being virtually irrelevant.

A few brigades had sound-detector devices such as vibraphones and trapped-persons locators, which pick up voices, tapping sounds and, in some circumstances, the noise of breathing, through sensors lowered into rubble. Trials in London with the trapped-persons locator, made in Israel, have revealed many difficulties in filtering out unwanted sounds such as the noise of underground trains. In theory, at least, they are more useful than thermal-imaging cameras, but it is hard to find any records in Britain of rescues that could be attributed to their use.

Although fire brigades in Britain do not keep them, the Home Office report also looked at the use of search-and-rescue dogs which are specially trained for urban rescue, like those the RAF had in the Second World War. Since the mid-1980s, the Americans have organized a national rescue service to attend major incidents and dogs are favoured by their specialist teams. Among its evaluations of high-tech equipment, the Home Office report contains this extract from an account by Chase Sargent, battalion chief and paramedic with Virginia Beach Fire Department, on an exercise involving the US disaster search dog team.

If heavy rescue team personnel are unable to locate and pinpoint the victims of a building collapse, their skills have been wasted. With the main emphasis to find, treat and remove victims, locating

113

them quickly and in time is essential. Search dogs and their handlers provide the edge needed to gain maximum live extrications from building collapses. Dog teams have proven effective time and time again in building search-and-rescue functions across the world . . . additional search functions such as infrared cameras, listening devices, bore-hold cameras [a fibre-optic device] and other electronic sensing equipment are interesting if you have them in your area. But in this author's opinion they will never replace a dog's nose and a knowledgeable handler.

The inescapable conclusion of this Home Office report, as well as the evidence from abroad and the experience of fire brigades which have tried out thermal-imaging cameras at real incidents is that there are no technological wonders which have revolutionized search and rescue in collapsed buildings. Most success comes from the old method of calling for silence and listening, although its limitations are brought home by the case of the two women buried for four days during the Blitz because their voices could not be heard.

Fire brigades have thermal-imaging cameras for training in firefighting and for their occasional use in looking for the seats of fires or detecting 'hot spots'. If their only function were searching for bodies in collapsed buildings, they would not be worth the cost of buying and training firefighters to use them. However, once they have these cameras, brigades naturally take them along to all kinds of incidents just in case they can be of some help.

Yet the interest in the presence of these cameras at the Putney gas explosion of January 1985 had some bizarre repercussions. It suggested to countries which suffer terrible death tolls from natural disasters, such as earthquakes, that the British firefighter now had a piece of equipment which could magically transform the painstaking task of digging in the rubble of flattened cities. It so happened that one of the many firefighters who went to the Putney incident came from

Gibraltar and spoke Spanish. Joe Bishop was not directly involved with the rescue there, nor in the use of thermal-imaging cameras, but he was persuaded by his superiors to give an interview to a Spanish-speaking TV crew who had turned up to cover the story, and naturally he mentioned the cameras.

Word of the new wonder camera spread across Central and South America, and when later the same year Mexico suffered a terrible earthquake an appeal was made, via the Home Office, for London firefighters to fly out with their equipment to help search for survivors. It was an era in which the export to developing countries of British medical and other expertise was becoming voguish, and Joe Bishop and a small team found themselves propelled from a gas explosion in Putney to the unimaginably worse scene of devastation in Mexico, armed with eleven thermal-imaging cameras.

'Thermal-imaging cameras were our ticket to Mexico,' says Bishop, 'but to be honest, in my experience they were not much use. What we could do had more to do with organizing people, command and control.' This first trip abroad was poorly organized on the spur of the moment, and in many respects farcical – the firefighters had no proper uniforms and in the end had to borrow some from the wardrobe of a Mexican lieutenant-colonel.

But there have been subsequent visits, and there is now an established system whereby firefighters in Britain can volunteer for service overseas, arranged through the Home Office. But for the most part it is not the thermal-imaging camera that is at the forefront of the firefighter abroad so much as his or her 'jack-of-all-trades' skills. The last major expedition was to the Kurdish refugee camps in northern Iraq, where firefighters built field hospitals and laid on emergency water supplies.

In world terms, the British firefighter is not an expert in collapsed-structure rescue for the very good reason that it is a skill that is rarely called upon. It would be absurd for fire services in Britain to train search-and-rescue dogs, for example, for the few times they would ever be used. There are voluntary organizations such as SARDA, the Search and Rescue Dogs Association, which might provide a service, but both handlers and hounds would need special urban rescue training to be effective.

By and large, then, contemporary collapsed-structure rescue operations will not be very different from the wartime rescues fifty years ago. Because firefighters carry much better and more powerful cutting and jacking equipment to deal with extrication at road and rail accidents, the task of getting through to a casualty can be easier in some circumstances – it all depends on the type of building, and the type of collapse.

Glasgow, which suffered the terrible Clarkston disaster in 1971, has had its fair share of building collapses since. The most recent to catch the headlines was the spectacular disintegration of one of the city's century-old tenement blocks, which came tumbling down at 10:30am on the morning of 29 March 1993. This was not due to a gas explosion but to a structural problem caused by weakened foundations.

According to the *Glasgow Evening Times* of that day, 'Using sophisticated heat-seeking equipment' firemen managed to locate a woman trapped in the rubble. It is quite true that the Strathclyde Fire Brigade did take thermal-imaging cameras to the ruined tenement block at Springfield Road, in the Parkhead district of the city, and did use them to search for bodies, dead or alive. But they played no part in the remarkable rescue of the fifty-five-year-old American woman who, as it turned out, was the only person trapped in the block when it collapsed.

Firefighter Keith MacGillvery recalls:
We were faced with a large pile of rubble and it was unclear how many people were involved or what had happened. The building was in a dangerous condition, and we were worried about how the collapse had occurred. We cleared the area and got the gas board in because there was a smell of gas.

We could only guess that there might

be somebody in the building, and we started listening probably after about five minutes. There were thirteen or fourteen of us shouting and listening, and it was a couple of minutes before we heard a woman's voice and she was able to give her name. We set up teams to remove the debris on top and had safety teams to look out for the building above, because there were high winds. We cleared the top layers of debris where there was a lot of pipework and steel, and it probably took about an hour to get down to see her. For the rest of the time we could see she was trapped by the shoulders, body and legs, but she had not suffered any serious injuries.

One crew went to see if there was a way through to her from underneath, but at the end of the day it was a matter of removing all the debris and this took two or three hours. We used a lot of equipment we use for road-traffic accidents, inflatable shields and Acrow props. One firefighter went into the hole and kept up a conversation with her because we were concerned about the time it was taking to get her out and frightened she might go into unconsciousness. There were medical teams standing by.

In many ways the Strathclyde team was better equipped than the firefighters who went to Clarkston in 1971 as they had the cutting and propping gear acquired since the 1970s for heavy rescue at train crashes and road accidents. But the sophisticated detection gear did not play a part. 'We did not have listening devices,' MacGillvery says. 'The vibraphone was not available. We had the infrared camera and we did try to use it, but there was so much rubble and the heat source of a body is so little that it was no use to us.'

The rescue work – painstaking, traditional hard labour – eventually resulted in the woman, who had been visiting a relative in Glasgow, being taken out on a stretcher, amazingly without any serious injury.

Strathclyde Fire Service has taken a new

Much was was made in the press about the use of thermal-imaging cameras in the the rescue of a woman trapped when a tenement building collapsed in Glasgow in 1991. But she was found because she called out to rescuers, not because of any new technology.

interest in collapsed-building rescue, setting up a working party to study techniques and equipment because of the fear of a massive disaster such as an air crash on a big city like London or Glasgow. And indeed, the Lockerbie disaster of 1988, when a plane with 259 people on board was blown to pieces by a bomb and rained down bodies and pieces of aircraft on the small town, happened not far from Glasgow itself. At Lockerbie eight people on the ground were killed and several houses partially demolished. A similar explosion over a big city would be much more catastrophic, necessitating the search of rubble on a scale not experienced since the war.

If that were to happen it would present the emergency services with a uniquely challenging and horrific task, for there would be not only a high death toll, but a tremendous strain on the rescue workers themselves. However hardened firefighters, ambulance workers, police and emergency medical teams become to routine human suffering, disasters confront them with a mental stress on a different plane.

In the last war, rescue workers who were mere volunteers had to cope with scenes of obscene ghastliness, as have the emergency services since, from the Harrow train crash of 1952 to the Kegworth air disaster of 1989. But it is only in the past ten years or so that anybody has given much thought to the psychological and emotional impact this might have on rescue workers. A recognition that those people's lives might be seriously affected by their experiences, and that they may need protection from the horrors, has been one of the most dramatic changes in the work of the emergency services since the war.

CHAPTER SIX
AFTERSHOCK

On the cold morning of Friday 28 February 1975, just before 9am, City of London policeman Ray Jenkins was on pedestrian patrol duty near Moorgate tube station when he got a call telling him that a train had run into the buffers at the end of a line. He went to take a look. 'It was an excuse to get off school crossing patrol. I went into the station – it was rush hour and there weren't many people about, and the staff were standing around looking a bit vacant. It struck me as strange.'

I went down the escalator. I could see down the length of the platform and there were a few people lying on it. I was expecting the train to be on the buffers, but as I looked to my left into the tunnel I saw that this train had gone right up. It was an absolute shock. Very few people were going to be alive – I knew

Firemen working to free people trapped in the Moorgate tube disaster of 1975 witnessed some horrific scenes, but few admitted to any emotional difficulties afterwards.

that in a split second.

PC Jenkins, then twenty-six years old, was one of the first rescue workers to discover what turned out to be the worst peacetime disaster in the history of London Underground. What had started out as an ordinary morning, helping children across the road ended with him involved in a nightmare 52ft below the city streets. The Metropolitan Police recruiting slogan of the time, 'Dull it isn't,' was a grotesque understatement in this case: very few ordinary police officers could ever expect to experience anything like the horrors of the Moorgate tube disaster in their whole careers.

Moorgate is a busy interchange in the city, the gateway to the heart of London's financial capital for commuters from suburbs to the north, south, east and west. What was then the Northern City tube line ended at Moorgate, whereas on other tube lines the station was simply a stop. That morning a six-carriage train had left the Victorian station above ground at Drayton Park at 8.39am, with driver Leslie Newson at the controls. The journey to Moorgate took only a few minutes, the train calling at three other stations on its short run into the city. By the time it left the last stop, Old Street, the station before Moorgate, it had about 300 passengers on board, many of them crammed into the front three coaches – the train was heading for Platform 9, where the exit is near the front, and regular commuters in a hurry put up with the discomfort of the crowded front carriages to get away quickly when the train pulled in.

As the train emerged from the darkness of the tunnel into the bright lights of Platform 9 it should have been rapidly slowing down. The passengers sensed that something was wrong. A guard on the platform momentarily saw the face of driver Leslie Newson, staring straight ahead, as the train shot by at 40mph. He never applied the brakes, and when his body was recovered four days later from the tangled wreckage it was clear that he had not even put up his hands to protect himself. Still gripping the 'dead man's handle' which, if released, would have automatically jammed on the brakes, Newson drove the 8.39 from Drayton Park straight into a short tunnel at the end of the platform, where it buckled and concertinaed as it went over a 'sand drag' – a safety device designed to stop a train if it overshot the platform – and hit the buffers embedded in a 5ft thick concrete wall.

The dead-end tunnel in which three tube carriages packed with commuters were rammed into each other when the driver inexplicably drove into the buffers at full speed.

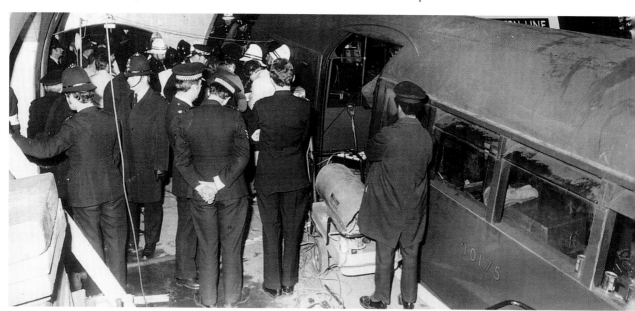

What happened to the driver in those last few seconds nobody knows: his train was mechanically sound; he had not been drinking; he was a quiet, apparently happy, family man about to buy his daughter a car. The conclusion drawn was that he must have suffered some kind of seizure. Newson would have been killed instantly when his head smashed through the glass at the front of the cab, and so would some of the passengers in the first three coaches. The impact compressed the first coach by half its normal length as it jack-knifed on the rails; the second carriage rode over the back of it, and the third, its front half concealed in the short tunnel and the back still protruding into the platform, rammed into the rear of the second. The last three coaches were relatively undamaged, all the impact having been absorbed by the first three. People were thrown about in these back carriages, but some of them got out of the train and went to work without even realizing that a terrible disaster had occurred at the front of the train.

It took a while to raise the alarm, and for nearly fifteen minutes the rest of Moorgate Station carried on as if nothing had happened: the underground tunnels and platforms are all isolated from one another and the noise of the crash had been insulated by the tunnel. Even the guard on the platform who had seen the train shoot by at speed did not understand at first the awfulness of the situation. He simply called London Transport headquarters to report that a train had hit the buffers and that the driver might be hurt. This message was relayed to the ambulance service, who called nearby Bart's Hospital.

Outside in the street a passer-by told a City of London police motorcyclist that there had been an accident in the station and he went to take a look. But nobody had told the station staff in the booking hall about it, and the patrolman wandered around until he found the almost unbelievably gruesome scene on Platform 9, where survivors were emerging covered in black dust. He was joined there by PC Ray Jenkins. While the patrolman went back up to report a major accident, Jenkins

At Moorgate it took three days to cut away the carriages and recover all the bodies, including that of the train driver.

joined a crew of firefighters and a doctor in an exploration of the carriages buried deep in the tunnel.

A message reached the nearest fire station, at the Barbican, reporting that at 8.57, there was an accident at Moorgate with 'persons trapped'. Station Officer Chris Wood and his crew raced to the scene. He recalls:

When we arrived at Moorgate no rail staff knew where the accident was. We got down to platform 9, and the platform was empty. There were a few staff there and I asked something like, 'What you got, mate?' They said the train had gone into the tunnel, which was a dead end. There were only three carriages standing at the end of the platform. I used to travel on this line, and I didn't remember it being as short as three carriages, so I assumed the rest of the train had entered the tunnel. It was dead quiet. I squeezed between the tunnel wall and the wrecked coaches and worked my way along the tunnel. As the light of my torch shone into the carriages, people started calling out. We went into the third coach: it was such a confined space, and there were people crushed, dead, others calling and some just quiet, who were maybe the worst injured. And as other crews arrived we just started getting people out.

PC Jenkins joined the fire crew in the train. *I was quite skinny then. A thin fireman, a thin doctor and I cut our way into the wreck. Once in there you couldn't get out, because space was so confined, and we were passing the injured back along the coach. It was the worst thing I had seen that far in my career. We had had the Old Bailey bomb blast, but this was worse because there were so many people. It was very intense: they were all around you and the metal of the carriages had crushed through faces and bodies. People were trapped halfway up their bodies with so much weight on them that you knew they wouldn't survive. The coroner told everyone at the inquest that all the dead died instantly and wouldn't have suffered. Anyone who knows anything about disasters knows that is a load of cobblers. It gave everyone a lot of comfort, though.*

From 9am until 9pm, when the last survivors were cut from the wreckage, the rescue work went on, the firefighters stripped to the waist in temperatures which rose to 100 degrees Fahrenheit as they hacked and sawed their way through the carriages in the close, constricted and airless tunnel. PC Jenkins and Station Officer Wood worked until lunchtime on that Friday, by which time they were completely exhausted. They were relieved by other crews, crawling like miners through the hideous ghost train where commuters, killed where they stood, stared horribly at them as they comforted the dying and encouraged

those with a chance of survival. The very last rescue deeply affected many of the firefighters and others involved. In the front carriage a young woman, Margaret Liles, was on her way to work on her first day as a policewoman when the crash happened, was trapped in a tiny space among dead bodies with a young man, also alive, lying across her. For hours firefighters worked to free them both, at first thinking that if they got the man out they could release the policewoman, and then finding that the two were so intertwined that this was not possible.

Finally, after several consultations with doctors, a surgeon was called for and the terrible decision had to be taken to amputate

Getting in and out of the carriages at Moorgate was difficult, and firefighters had to cut through the tangle of metal to reach survivors.

the woman's foot. She was pinned by a girder they could not cut through, and unless she was freed neither survivor could be released. She was to survive, and later to marry and bring up a family, but the young man, cheerful throughout his ordeal, died a few days later.

The completion of the rescue operation was not the end of the Moorgate nightmare. Somehow, the carriages with their grim cargo of corpses had to be removed from the tunnel. At this stage it was vital that every piece of evidence that might give some indication of the cause of the crash should be preserved, and simply to haul the carriages out might have destroyed some vital clues. So the wreck was cut up bit by bit until the workers reached the body of driver Leslie Newson at the front.

This took four days, during which the decomposing bodies of the dead became more and more putrid in the heat of the tunnel and rescue workers had to be issued with protective clothing and undergo decontamination when they took a break. As they cut through the wreckage the death toll rose until it finally reached forty-one, to add to seventy-six injured. Two people taken alive from the train died later.

In all, 1,324 firefighters, eighty ambulance workers, 240 police officers and sixteen doctors, as well as many other support workers such as the WRVS and the Salvation Army, were involved at some stage in the Moorgate disaster. For most, what they witnessed would be the worst thing they had ever seen, or were likely to see, in their entire careers. Twenty years ago little thought was given to the possibility that any of those rescue workers might find it difficult to cope with what they had experienced. Nobody denied that it was a nightmare, of course, but professionals like police officers, firefighters and ambulance workers were expected to treat it as part of their work and get on with their jobs. Nobody talked about post-traumatic stress disorder (PTSD) in rescue workers, for the term did not exist. It was coined by American psychologists in 1980 and was not current in the emergency services in Britain until very recently. Nobody

thought about suing London Transport for subjecting them to damaging psychological stress, although in law they might have had a case to pursue. More recently, the courts have awarded compensation to rescue workers, although the legal logic of who is and who is not eligible is hard to follow.

If the same disaster happened tomorrow it would be very different. All the services would be on the lookout for rescuers who might suffer some kind of breakdown; there would be counselling available, debriefing sessions, concern from welfare officers. And the rescuers themselves would be aware that they might suffer flashbacks, sleeplessness, tearfulness, or an inability to cope which could affect their careers.

The point has been made that, of all the changes in the emergency services since the last war, the acceptance of PTSD has been one of the most profound. It has happened only in the last ten years and still provokes bitter reactions from some of the old hands, who regard the whole idea that they might not be able to cope with the horrors of disasters as ridiculous. For them the entire paraphernalia of psychological debriefing is just another money-spinning nonsense which interferes with and undermines the solid old principles of stalwartness in which they take some pride.

And the implication is, of course, that in the past, before post-traumatic stress disorder was recognized as a real and damaging medical problem, many rescue workers did suffer from it and should have been helped. It is not possible here to resolve such a complex issue, and indeed it is one on which there is still very considerable disagreement among psychiatrists and psychologists as well as in the emergency services themselves. Recently concern has been voiced that amateurish debriefing could make things worse, undermining the little-understood defence mechanisms and means of coping which rescue workers develop naturally, and transforming something thought of as a 'normal' reaction into a medical condition. It cannot be disputed, in fact, that though there may have been in the past 'hidden' psychological casualties of disaster among rescue workers, most of them find ways of coming to terms with what they have experienced without taking to drink, going sick, suffering marital breakdowns or enduring any of the other long-term and serious consequences of a failure to cope.

Nobody has studied the aftershock effects on those rescue workers who went to Moorgate, but the testimony of a few of them suggests that there were then, as there must be now, many different ways of dealing with such an experience.

Chris Wood, now retired from the fire service and living in a rural part of Norfolk, has this to say about his own reactions to Moorgate.

I had never experienced anything like that, but in those days you just got on with the job. To be quite honest, you don't think about it until afterwards. We were just doing the carriages, pulling people out, and we were working from 9am until 12.30pm. You were so exhausted that when you were pulling someone it would feel more like they were pulling you. We were reluctant to come out because we had got a system going, but in the end we had to give up as the relief crews arrived. We went back to the station, talked about it a bit and had a cup of tea. Usually you either laugh or cry about these things, but nobody cried that I remember, and certainly nobody laughed. Nobody went sick on my crew, or had any traumas, or came to see me about it. In those days it was considered part of the job: you expected to find difficult things.

It did not affect me in any way. I never really brought any fire-brigade business home. I didn't talk about it, I never had any sleepless nights or headaches or days off – that idea wasn't about in those days, you weren't expected not to be able to cope. Nowadays if you fall over you are thinking about compensation. This trauma thing is big business – it is the in thing.

As you get older you remember things more. Maybe I'll get post-traumatic stress disorder when I am ninety.

Wood's attitude, hard and uncompromising as it may seem, represents the view of probably the great majority of firefighters who joined the service twenty or thirty years ago. Moreover, stress counsellors generally agree that of all rescue workers, it is the firefighters who are most reluctant to acknowledge traumatic stress.

It is quite possible that this is not because they hide their feelings but because of the way they approach their job. They tease each other and indulge in a good deal of black humour, all of which is much too gruesome to repeat to a lay audience – their ghoulish jokes could easily be misunderstood as callousness, when in fact such behaviour is recognized as a release, a legitimate and possibly effective way of dealing with stress. They, more than other rescue teams, work in small crews who stick together and rely on each other for survival when situations become dangerous. They are usually the first on the scene of a disaster and are exposed to the horrors of road accidents and fatal fires quite frequently. When their job is done they climb back into their fire engine and go back to the station together, where they have a cup of tea and change out of their gear. It is not that firefighters do not suffer: they do, but they are close-knit, and many studies of PTSD in rescue workers suggest that camaraderie is an important factor in the management of stress.

Fireman Richard Furlong (now retired), who was twenty-six years old at the time of Moorgate, came with the crew from Shoreditch Fire Station and was one of the first into the train. When he was called to Moorgate, he knew it was a big accident, and he did not want to miss it. 'Everybody wanted to go. Your heart starts pumping and the adrenaline starts flowing. We proceeded down the platform to be met by all the people coming up towards us, black and blue.' While the other crew was working in the second and third coaches, Furlong went towards the front.

The front was eight or nine feet up. All I had was a hand torch, and I'm the first person these people have seen – you feel so inadequate. There's not a murmur, it's deathly silent and you ask yourself, what do I do? You talk to them, you say, 'We're here now, we'll get you out.' I sent a message back – there were no radios, it was all by word of mouth – 'There's a bit of a problem: there's another load up here.'

In the front coach, squashed up to the ceiling, there was a young couple. They were getting married soon afterwards. I sat down and took my tunic off and told them, 'I'm not going until all you lot are out.' But I was ordered out in the end.

I spent five and a half hours there in the morning and went back again for four and a half hours in the afternoon. I had people dying in front of me, but we did rescue a lot of people too. I had been in the brigade since I was sixteen, and I was at the peak of my fitness and my experience. I wish it hadn't happened, but as it did occur, I was grateful that I had been there to experience it. I would not have wanted to miss it.

I got back to the station and stood under the shower and cried my heart out.

Firefighters are used to death and suffering, but the conditions at Moorgate were the worst most had ever seen or were likely to see again.

It was the feeling of helplessness. From there, basically, I never went back. My guv'nor said, 'You have done enough – you don't need to go back if you don't want to,' and I didn't fancy it.

None of us talked about Moorgate at length. We were a bit shell-shocked. It was one of those things you did to the best of your ability. All you could say was you did your bit and it wasn't enough. People who were not on duty wanted to hear about it, but I wouldn't have said it was a mess-table topic of conversation.

Obviously, you wonder about the people you couldn't get to. When there's a good fire and no one's hurt, you all talk it over, but the seriousness and the traumatic effect Moorgate had on people meant they didn't talk so much about that.

I didn't tell my wife the details. I had two young children at the time. Help was non-existent – there was no such thing as stress. You did your job, which was what you were paid for, and you learned not to *show your emotions. It was looked on as a sign of weakness. I have the ability to put it behind me and cut it off, but you can never forget about it. I can vividly recall it now. If the counselling is there people will use it. I wouldn't have dreamed of going to the doctor and saying, 'I have been at this accident,' but obviously the stress was there, and the counselling must be beneficial to those who receive it.*

None of the firefighters want to say that what they experienced was easy to handle, or that it was not traumatic. What they do want to say is that each of them had to find a way of coping: some shut it out, some remember; some talk to their wives and friends, others do not. At Moorgate quite a number of young firefighters were 'blooded' by their superiors – deliberately sent in to see dead bodies,

asked to pick up severed limbs.

Firefighter Chris Reynolds was twenty-four years old when he went to Moorgate from Paddington Fire Station as part of an emergency tender crew whose job it was to cut out survivors. His experience at the disaster was frankly shocking.

I can remember the layout down there, and a chap sitting up with his briefcase in his hand, off to work, and one of those bogeys [wheels] sticking though his chest. The bodies were wedged so tight; they were packed in solid, pushed in like sardines. When you know you are going to see something horrific you prepare yourself for it. You strengthen up your character inside. If I was walking along and something happened unexpectedly, I should think I would be as shocked as anyone else. But you detach yourself.

When I was cutting people out, I had to sit on a young girl's head, using her head and neck like a seat. She was dead. People were standing up, dead, staring at us. We couldn't take that so we pinned up a salvage sheet over them. But as a team of men you work together, and you are sometimes callous. That's the cruel part, the black humour. We cut into the driver's cabin and we found his sandwiches and someone offered them round.

The stench! You can't stop your physical reactions. One sad thing was the people waiting up the top to see their loved ones who had been killed. The coffins were lined up but bodies swell up and we couldn't get them in the coffins. There's no dignity in death, it's just dead meat. Parents would never recognize their sons and daughters.

Firefighters take a breather after working for hours below ground at Moorgate.

Moorgate was so vivid. Walking on bodies is a very hard thing, like walking on jelly, you're slip sliding because it's like muscle really. I'm a strong character, I was the main plank of the station.

Reynolds remembers that the 'blooding' of young recruits was routine, although he did not know anybody to whom it had happened at Moorgate. 'You have to see mangled, burned bodies. You stick the youngest down there, and get them to have a good look around, and they have acquired something. Being in the fire service and never having seen a body is like being a bloke and never having had sex. The more you see, the more experience you have.' Of his own experiences, Reynolds says:

When you came back from the incident it affected you. You kept seeing images, you were walking on bodies. But it never affected me mentally or changed my life. 'You've got to be built of cobalt steel' – that's what we used to say. We used to play on it: we were the 'glitter boys', we had so many awards and commendations for rescuing people – because we had all the hotel fires around Paddington, you see – awards all up on the wall. You will never find a shy fireman or someone who's insecure – they would be gobbled up by the watch. Men can be so cruel to each other, although this has been stamped out because there are women in the service now.

Reynolds did take the Moorgate story, or some of it, home. 'I talked to my wife about what I saw, but it's only you who can put it in a little box in the back of your head and get on with life; shelve it, put it away and say, "It's another job." Of course it's traumatic, but you get over it.'

Those firefighters who were prepared to talk about the disaster to their wives acknowledge the support that gave them. Indeed, families have almost certainly been the most significant unofficial, unpaid counsellors over the years. George Hull, a sub-officer with the emergency tender crew from Islington, saw some of the worst of Moorgate.

It is still vivid, particularly the image of the last people trapped inside, still sitting in their seats, legs and arms sticking out. A row of people still sitting in their seats. It must have been very quick for them. I'm not cynical, and wouldn't knock the support given nowadays because some people do need it, but I do think there is a bit of hype about it. At the end of the day, the emergency services person is a professional and has to be able to deal with it.

My wife was absolutely great. In the summer especially I would go and sit out on the patio and she would bring me a cup of tea and then just leave me, and when I was ready I would come in. She would know when something was affecting me. She was very involved with the brigade – she was part of it too, in many ways. If I needed to talk she would sit and listen.

George Hull retired in 1993 after twenty-eight years' service. There were other incidents in his career that affected him more than that disaster – seeing two of his men killed in a fire when a wall collapsed, for example, and incidents involving children.

PC Ray Jenkins, who worked alongside the firefighters in the Moorgate train, had a very different experience from them afterwards. He was not part of a close-knit crew like the firemen.

I was down there for about four hours, from 9am until about lunchtime, and then I came back to the station and changed because I was soaked in blood and oil. We were given bags to put our clothes in, and they were sealed and destroyed. I put on a fresh uniform and was called up by my chief who said, 'Take two days off.'

I don't think they knew then about the effects, though there was the feeling that if you weren't shocked, you should be, and they sent you away. The first day I went into the countryside. You just wanted to cry all the time. People you knew didn't want you to talk about it, it was so horrible. You were just left alone.

PC Jenkins believes his chief had read a circular sent around after a plane crash at which some police officers had reacted badly, and that it recommended that traumatized police be given time off. (This would have been the air disaster at Stockport, Manchester in 1967. As police went to the rescue the plane burst into flames, and they could only watch as the survivors of the crash were burned alive.) But in his two days away he missed the company of others who had been at the disaster.

I was a single man, living in single quarters. When I came back and mixed with the other blokes, it was better. Twenty years on you are told to talk about it. Once I came back to work it was OK. You do get flashbacks, but nothing for the first couple of weeks. After that, something prompts it and you see the faces of people hopelessly trapped for quite a while. I can recall quite a lot of detail.

PC Jenkins does not feel he has suffered any long-term effects, and in some ways he has seen worse since. The police are, however, especially vulnerable to stress, for reasons explored later.

A number of studies have been made of the stress suffered by ambulance workers, but none relating specifically to Moorgate. Hearsay evidence suggests that some did leave the service because of their experiences there, though others feel they coped with it, hard as it was. Roy Kitchen was an in-service training officer at the time. He picked up news of Moorgate on his staff-car 'urgent' radio. 'I had not been called to the job,' he remembers, 'but I found myself going faster and faster. Then I picked up the instinct that this was a major, and I put the lights on and the two-tone and just then I heard that the London Hospital was going to be one of the designated hospitals, so I made my way there.' Roy Kitchen's car was then commandeered as his radio was needed, and he was taken to

Moorgate in a police car.

Everything was very quiet and organized, there was no panic. I said, 'Where's it all happening?' and someone replied, 'In the tunnel.' It was really amazing – to get to the coalface, as it were, you had to go along into the train, then out of it, along the track, then get in the train again. It was like a rabbit warren, and black, totally black. The fire brigade later set up a couple of free-standing floodlights, but the lighting at that stage was from torches. Professionalism takes over – you go on to automatic pilot. Obviously it was major news at the time, but I didn't read the newspaper reports after it happened. I didn't get involved, I just switched off. I think that was my way of dealing with it.

I remember later in the afternoon getting back to Romford and just sitting there, and people asking what it was like. I said: 'Just a bloody mess.' Only talking about it now do I realize how I shut off. I remember feeling ill; I felt funny when I came out and the doctors gave us these salt tablets. I can remember feeling these things going down and exploding in me – it was really vile. It was probably the worst job I have been involved with. It was the conditions that made it the worst.

Roy Kitchen, now aged sixty-two and retired, went back to Moorgate Station two years ago to try to get an idea of where it all happened. But 'I didn't have any stress from it,' he says. 'My experience at Moorgate stood me in good stead training people later.'

As gruesome as it was, the Moorgate disaster did not appear to make any of the rescue workers feel guilty about those they could not save, as is sometimes the case in such situations. The firefighters were frustrated when the blades of the Cengar saws kept breaking, the ambulance crew wished they had had better communications, and not everything went wonderfully smoothly, but the overwhelming impression that remains is that they all did their best with the tools they had, and a pretty good job in extremely difficult circumstances. In theory, at least, this is likely to have reduced the amount of stress and trauma experienced afterwards, for all disasters have their own unique kind of 'ethos' which influences how rescue workers respond to them.

In 1989 PC Ray Jenkins attended the *Marchioness* disaster, when a pleasure boat carrying a party of young people on the Thames was hit by a freighter. Although he had seen people die before his eyes at Moorgate, there was nothing he could have done for them. It was different with the *Marchioness*.

> *That was a nightmare. People were hanging on to buoys and we were calling out for them to hold on, help was coming, and no help came. The others were all trapped and were going to die. At Moorgate you were very busy doing positive things. You had no regrets because you did everything you could. With the* Marchioness, *people were dying as you watched: it was all still going on when the police first got there.*

The fact that the Hillsborough football stadium disaster, which happened nearly a quarter of a century after Moorgate, attracted so much attention from counsellors and led to thirty-seven police officers suing their own chief constable for compensation because of the trauma they suffered, is not simply a result of a fashionable interest in post-traumatic stress disorder. True, if it had happened twenty-five years ago there would have been no counselling, and it is unlikely that any police officers would have sued for compensation, but there would certainly still have been a degree of trauma which might have been beyond the scope of 'old-fashioned' methods of coping.

The study of post-traumatic stress is still in its infancy, although human emotional and psychological reactions to exceptionally disturbing events, such as fires, earthquakes, shipwrecks and all manner of calamities, must have existed since time immemorial. In this century, the First World War left hundreds of thousands of soldiers, many of whom were not professionals but volunteers, suffering from what was called 'shell-shock'. Often the symptoms – anxiety, flashbacks, depression, a sense of vulnerability and guilt – emerged long after the horror of the trenches was past. Although it was assumed that the mental breakdown of soldiers was due to the constant bombardments they suffered, the generic term 'shell-shock' could equally well apply to those who suffered from the hideous conditions in the trenches, seeing bodies blown to pieces, friends gunned down and dying in agony.

Although post-traumatic stress disorder was not given its name until 1980, it seeks to describe the symptoms that literally millions of people must have suffered over the centuries: an inability to come to terms with a horrific experience and to return to a 'normal' lifestyle. While it has long been accepted that those directly involved in disasters, the survivors of plane crashes or the relatives of those who have died, are likely to suffer serious mental stress, it is only much more recently that it has been widely acknowledged that the same problems might arise among rescue workers attending such scenes.

This is for the very obvious and understandable reason which has emerged in many of the reports of rescue workers at Moorgate: it is expected that those who choose to take up a line of work in which they are bound to be exposed to scenes of terrible human suffering will be able to cope. A surgeon who fainted at the sight of blood would not be much good in the operating theatre, just as a firefighter who cannot deal with handling charred bodies is not going to be of help at fires. All emergency workers will, at some time in their careers, witness gruesome sights that most people would find stomach-churning and unbearable. If they cannot cope with these experiences they have to give up the job. The phrase 'If you can't stand the heat, stay out of the kitchen' is often quoted among rescue workers themselves.

It is a reasonable assumption, then, that emergency workers are in this sense 'self-selected': that they are not ordinary people who happen to be doing unusually stressful jobs, but choose to do these stressful jobs because they find them fulfilling. When there is a 'major', a disaster, they become excited, the adrenaline rush carries them on, and they *want* to be there, not to avoid what could turn out to be one of the most demanding experiences of their lives.

Throughout this book, rescue workers describing their first realization that they were dealing with something exceptional, and that they might, through their efforts and skill, save someone's life, talk about excitement. It is not that they relish scenes of appalling suffering, rather that they are driven by a desire to go to the rescue and a disaster presents the ultimate challenge. Afterwards they might feel they could have done better, that their organization was faulty, that another life could have been saved if they had had a particular piece of equipment. But they still want to be there.

Those who went to the rescue at the Clapham train crash, to the Kegworth air disaster, to the Putney gas explosion or to Moorgate felt that thrill. It is probably felt strongest by firefighters, much of whose lives are spent waiting for something to happen, like soldiers before a battle. When they do go to the rescue for real, they are quickly in the thick of it. Ambulance workers feel that too, but in a different way, because, being medics, they tend to feel more directly responsible for saving lives. Their work is less clear-cut than that of firefighters: they have to keep casualties alive, if they can, and make difficult medical judgements, sometimes over a long period of time.

It is the police who are likely to be in the most ambiguous position, because at disasters their primary function is not to rescue, although they might become involved. They are likely to be bystanders, watching the rescue work going on and guarding it, rather than doing it themselves. Their job is often to keep crowds back, to control things, to collect evidence and to pick up the pieces – bits of body, personal belongings, broken wreckage –

afterwards; a doleful task at the best of times. Like Ray Jenkins at Moorgate, the ordinary copper on the beat might go from a school crossing patrol straight to a train crash. At a major incident, police will be called in from a wide area and will very often not be part of a coherent crew like the firefighters are. This was the experience of PC Jenkins at Moorgate, as we have seen.

For all these reasons, police officers, or at least some of them, are probably particularly vulnerable at the scene of a disaster. A number of studies have shown that body recovery can lead to all kinds of mental stress, and those most likely to get through it without serious anxiety are members of specialist, volunteer teams who know what they are in for. Indeed, a study of one such team which went from the Metropolitan Police to help after the Lockerbie air crash showed that they appeared to suffer no traumatic stress at all.

All these factors are relevant to the catastrophe at Hillsborough football ground which took place on 15 April 1989. In many respects it was the most distressing disaster of all those considered in this book because it was so public: so many deaths and injuries happened before the eyes of football supporters, police and St John Ambulance members, as well as fathers and mothers and brothers and sisters who witnessed the carnage, powerless to do anything about it, not to mention thousands of television viewers. If post-traumatic stress disorder had not been defined about a decade before Hillsborough, someone would have had to have invented it to account for the repercussions it has had on the people involved in the tragedy. There is still a great deal of bitterness about what happened, both among Liverpool supporters, who lost loved ones in what was an entirely avoidable disaster, and among police and ambulance people, who feel they were put in an impossible position, forced to watch innocent men, women and children die while a football match was being played on the field behind them. Whereas there was little sense of guilt among the rescue workers at Moorgate, the whole of the Hillsborough tragedy is imbued with a deep-seated sense of culpability and failure.

None of the police, firefighters or ambulance workers who went to Moorgate were implicated in the cause of the tragedy. It happened because a driver failed to apply the brakes on the train. The only sense of guilt rescue workers might have had would have related to how well they felt they handled the incident.

Hillsborough, on the other hand, was very different. To begin with, the police were dealing with what was recognized as a potentially dangerous situation: a football crowd. It was their job to control it. All crowds are hazardous – in the Victorian period, when there were many theatre fires, most of the deaths occurred in the panic to get out. People were crushed to death by the weight of their own numbers. This has also happened with football crowds.

At Hillsborough the danger was on the terraces, where a mass of supporters stood huddled together. There were often surges among these crowds as people pushed forward, and spectators at the front might be forced on to the pitch. Fighting among fans was also a potential cause as people would try to move away from the conflict. At football matches there was always tension because of the possibility of panic and pitch invasions, and this affected police attitudes towards any disturbances they noticed in the crowd. They were much more wary at Hillsborough of the likelihood of violence in the crowd than of a possible calamity because of poor crowd control.

So the police at Hillsborough were in no way psychologically prepared to deal with a disaster, and many found it impossible to take in when it began to happen before their eyes. They were on the lookout for trouble of a different kind.

On Saturday 15 April 1989, Liverpool faced Nottingham Forest in the semi-final of the FA Cup – matches are always played on neutral territory so that no side has home advantage. The ground chosen was Sheffield Wednesday's Hillsborough stadium, which was regarded as suitably well designed and situated. As always, there was an argument about the allocation of tickets to the two teams, and which of them should be allotted which section of the ground, and the Liverpool fans thought they had been short-changed. But exactly the same game had been played the previous season at the same ground, and there was no reason to believe there would be any serious problems. There would be 50,000 ticket-holding spectators attending.

South Yorkshire Constabulary agreed to police the match as they had done the previous year. As well as the police, there were thirty St John Ambulance staff, as always, with four cadets along for the experience. The St John volunteers were there to deal with minor injuries, people taken suddenly ill or fainting, not as any precaution against possible disaster. At that time, although officers from the South Yorkshire Ambulance Service attended, it was not customary to have ambulances and crews standing by in any numbers. There might be crowd trouble, but the police and stewards could deal with that.

All in all, there was an astonishing number of police officers deployed for the match. The total of 1,122 included nearly a third of all policemen in South Yorkshire, as well as mounted police from Liverpool and Nottingham to help control the crowds from their home towns. Police were grouped into what are called 'serials' of eight to ten constables with a sergeant and an inspector, and each serial was given a specific task.

There was a carnival atmosphere as the crowds built up for the match and by all accounts it was pretty good-humoured. Peter Wells was the duty officer for the St John Ambulance on the day.

I had been at the game the year before and as I was walking around the ground before the kick-off someone from Pen 3 [where the disaster was to occur] shouted, 'Have you got any headache pills?' and I

131

shouted back: 'You won't need any when they score the first goal.' And there were two girls who remembered me because they had been there the year before with a young man who had twisted his ankle and I had treated him. They said I wouldn't be needed this time because he wasn't with them. That's what the atmosphere was like.

The pens at Hillsborough were a bit like cages, with a hefty high wire fence to keep the crowds from spilling on to the pitch and more fencing running at right angles to it to divide the terraces into sections. Liverpool ticket-holders going through the turnstiles at what is known as the Leppings Lane end to their allotted section of the terraces had a choice once they were through of which pen they went into. They could go straight on down a tunnel, or to their left, or to their right. The segregation of the terraces into pens had been introduced eight years earlier to stop a huge, composite crowd from forming a crush: in other words, it was intended to prevent the very calamity which eventually occurred.

Since this was an all-ticket match and it was known that the ground could hold the 50,000 spectators, the only real possible

These police officers lined up in the Hillsborough football stadium in Sheffield at first thought they were stopping a riot between rival fans. In fact, they were witness to one of the worst disasters in postwar history, in which 95 Liverpool fans were crushed to death.

---

danger lay in how the fans distributed themselves between the pens. They could not see the pens as they came through the turnstiles and so could not judge how full each of them was. Unless they were already familiar with the ground, they did not know which pen they would end up in once they had decided which route to take.

The police monitoring the crowd did know which pens were empty and which were getting full. Pens 3 and 4 were behind the goal, a position preferred to those on the side of the field. Supporters coming through the turnstiles had no sign to tell them which direction to take for different pens, but as the route to Pens 3 and 4 was straight ahead, the majority took this option anyway.

Just before the game was due to start, a large number of Liverpool fans, arriving later than they would have wished, became caught up in a scrum of people outside the ground anxious to get into the match. The crush built up outside the main Leppings Lane turnstiles through the sheer weight of numbers moving forward through a narrow entrance. The police outside feared that there might be casualties and asked if they could open a gate further down from the turnstiles, Gate C, to ease the pressure. It took a few minutes for the order to be given, and then Gate C was opened and the fans flooded through, relieved that the crush outside had been eased as it had been becoming unbearable.

Once inside, these latecomers were not directed to any particular pen but found their own way, and many of them took the obvious route straight ahead, down the tunnel to Pens 3 and 4, which were already uncomfortably packed. As lines of police officers on the lookout for trouble watched, the fans at the front next to the anti-hooligan fencing began to show signs of distress. The force of the crowds behind was crushing them so that their faces, pressed against the fence, became horribly distorted. Supporters at the back of the crowd, also feeling the pressure, began to escape by leaping up and grabbing the helping hands extended from the stand above them, which pulled them to safety.

The worst crush was in Pen 3, from which the only escape was a small gate at the front leading on to the pitch. Fans in adjoining pens sensed the alarm and began to shout to the police to open the gate and free those trapped at the front.

From elsewhere in the ground it was not at all clear what was happening, and the game had begun. Was it a riot? Just another episode of hooliganism? That was the expectation, and what many police officers and others assumed

to be the source of the disturbance. But those close to Pen 3 could see that people were being crushed to death with no way out. In the crowd, fathers pinned by their arms watched their sons' faces turn blue, fans who could no longer open their lungs to breathe fainted. And then the small gate in Pen 3 was opened, as well as a similar gate from Pen 4.

One of the most graphic accounts of what

The awful moment when the small gate was opened to release fans trapped in Pen 3. Police and by-standers tried to drag the crushed spectators through.

The horror of Hillsborough is written on the faces of supporters when, as the pressure of numbers built up, people were crammed into pens from which there was no escape.

happened next is contained in the judgement of Mr Justice Waller on the claims for compensation made later by twenty-three out of the original thirty-seven police officers for psychological damage caused by their experiences at Hillsborough. Their claim was against the Chief Constable of South Yorkshire, who accepted responsibility for the disaster, along with two other defendants, the football club and their engineering advisers. This is how Mr Justice Waller described the scene.

> Gates out of Pens 3 and 4 were only finally opened from three o'clock. The struggle to reach those open gates caused a horrendous blockage of bodies. The dead, the dying and the desperate became interwoven in the sump at the front of the pens, especially by the gates. Those with strength left clambered over others submerged in the human heap and tried to climb out over the fence. They were now helped by police and other fans, who hauled them up and over.

> The steps from the sump at Gateways 3 and 4 were so congested with bodies alive and dead that each had to be prised from the pile by the police. Initially, no officer took effective charge. A number of individual officers and fans worked frantically to free those trapped but the cageways were so narrow that only two or three could get at the entwined bodies . . .

More officers arrived from the gymnasium and elsewhere in the ground.

Many used their own initiative to help those laid out on the pitch, to assist in getting others over the fencing and to comfort the distressed. But some stood in groups near the perimeter fence not knowing what to do. They had been summoned in response to what was thought to be a threat to public order. What they found was a horrific scene of carnage, and some young officers were shocked into impotence by what they saw.

It was truly gruesome: the victims were blue, cyanotic, incontinent; their mouths open, vomiting; their eyes staring. A pile of dead bodies lay and grew outside Gate 3. Extending further and further on to the pitch, the injured were laid down and attempts made to revive them. More and more walking survivors flooded out on to the pitch as the players left. The scene was emotive and chaotic as well as gruesome. As the enormity of the disaster was realized, many of the fans milling about were bitter and hostile to the police, blaming them for what had happened. Officers were confronted, abused, spat upon and even assaulted.

Police, spectators – some of whom saw their

own children dead on the pitch – doctors who happened to be at the match and members of St John Ambulance did their best to revive those who were unconscious or already dead, giving mouth-to-mouth resuscitation to people who had vomited and choked and whose faces had turned blue. Peter Wells, the St John Ambulance duty officer, recalls:

> I was on the other side of the ground from the Leppings Lane end and we saw the fans coming over the fence. Someone said it was a pitch invasion, but I could see it wasn't and we went over. I was fortunate in the sense that I had been in the fire brigade – in fact I had only retired the day before – and I'd seen some pretty horrific sights. You must put the shutters down and get on with the job.
>
> I was on the pitch side of the fence where the fans were being crushed. I rushed back to the ambulance because I could see they needed oxygen, and just tore the mask off. I tried to give some oxygen to a girl by putting the tube in her throat but she died there before my eyes. It was one of the worst things I have ever seen. My wife was with me and she gave mouth-to-mouth resuscitation to some of the casualties. The St John people all did a wonderful job, despite the fact that people were vomiting and there was blood everywhere.

Police Sergeant Don Hill was in charge of a mobile patrol outside the ground when he received a series of messages saying there were problems with crowd control, and a final one instructing all police officers to go to the ground. This is an extract from the statement he made when claiming compensation.

> As I entered, I looked towards the Leppings Lane end and saw a large number of police officers and supporters standing on the playing area. The game had been stopped and I could see from the distance that people were climbing over the security fencing. I was still not fully aware of what the situation was, and from what I saw I assumed that a pitch invasion was taking place.
>
> I walked with my officers along the front of the North Stand, expecting to have to begin to move supporters either back into the Leppings Lane terraces or out of the ground. I then saw some of the crowd crushed against the security fence. People's faces were pinned against the meshing so that it looked like the meshing had stuck into their flesh. When we realized it was not an invasion, we tried to get people out as soon as possible.
>
> Everyone was pushing everyone else out of the way so that they could help. One chap had fallen, blocking the gateway, and we were trying to pull him out as there had been a domino effect of people falling over on top of him. We were pulling on his arms and eventually we did get him out, he was screaming and shouting at everyone so we assumed he was OK. We then went to try and pull people out of the gateway. At this time the people behind the fence, although in distress, were still in healthy colour. I did not think the situation was going to turn into a huge disaster. By the time we got the chap blocking the gate out of the way the situation behind the fence had deteriorated rapidly.
>
> The whole problem was the narrowness of the gate through which people had to pass. There were sufficient officers on the pitch to pull people away, but only two at a time could actually stand in the gateway. I continued to help as much as I could, but for much of the time I was standing helplessly watching people dying. Fans were becoming more and more distressed in the crowd and faces were going blue and purple.

Only a few police were involved in trying to drag spectators out of the pens. Many more helped as other supporters ripped down advertising hoardings to use as makeshift stretchers to carry them to the gymnasium at the ground, which was turned into a triage point and a mortuary. At 3pm, when the game kicked off, many police had been having their lunch there: less than an hour later they were detailed to attend to the bodies of those who had died, having them photographed and identified by frantic and grieving parents and friends. Only one South Yorkshire Metropolitan Ambulance Service vehicle got on to the pitch itself – all the others were outside taking the injured delivered on advertising hoardings.

'I am now angry about a lot of things,' says Don Hill. 'This anger has built up from the time of the disaster. I have been discharged from my duties suffering from stress disorder.'

Sergeant Hill is one of fourteen officers whose claim for compensation has been agreed, though the sum involved has not been settled. The claims of twenty-three other officers heard by Mr Justice Waller, whose account of the disaster is quoted earlier, were turned down, although an appeal has been made to the House of Lords. The distinction between the claims agreed and those defended does not appear to have turned purely on a judgement on the question of whether or not they suffered psychological trauma. It has to do with a legal principle about whether they could be compensated as 'rescuers' or not.

Because he was in the thick of it, trying to get people out, Hill was classed a rescuer. 'Money is immaterial,' he says. 'The way I justify it is simply this: it's against an insurance company, in effect, not against the police. It's to make the people who run the police realize that senior officers are responsible for the welfare of their men.' Hill retired from the force in 1990, suffering from PTSD, and has a medical pension which, he says, is enough to live on comfortably.

His reaction to what happened at Hillsborough began almost immediately.

When we got out of the ground the first thing I was concerned about was that everybody rang home and told their families they were OK. When I rang home myself it started to hit me. I spoke to my wife, Ann, and said, 'I'm OK,' but

then I choked up completely. I couldn't speak. Then it was the macho thing – I went back to the station. Once you're with them you don't let your emotions overcome you, and there was no release of any emotion on the day. We were there until about 2am discussing what had gone off. The main theme was the behaviour of the Liverpool supporters, some of the incidents we had seen on the pitch, the anti-social behaviour. [It should be noted here that Mr Justice Taylor, in his report on the Hillsborough tragedy, discounted misbehaviour by fans as a cause of the disaster.]

I came home between 2 and 3am. Ann was still waiting for me. Initially, I couldn't speak, I just cried for a good ten minutes. It was nothing in particular, just the general scene; the overwhelming scale of the disaster was too much to cope with. I wasn't so bad after that. The next day I went to work. I sat down and wrote a full account of what had gone off and we spent the rest of the day just discussing it.

Then, starting on the Monday, I was down for one week's holiday and we had a touring caravan and we went up to North Yorkshire. I had already booked it. On reflection, it wasn't a very good thing to do. It started to hit me. I spent the whole week staring at the wall, not really mentally capable of doing much at all. I never read a paper all week. Ann had been busy in the background ringing our son to say, 'Don't have any papers in the house when we get back.'

Before he went away, Hill had driven past Hillsborough Stadium and seen the flowers and scarves and teddy bears put there in memoriam. 'It was very upsetting seeing that. I still wasn't showing much emotion at all, I was simply in a daze, I had a couple of weeks off sick – my doctor gave me a note as I was suffering from reactive depression. During the next two weeks I improved considerably and got counselling from the people at work.

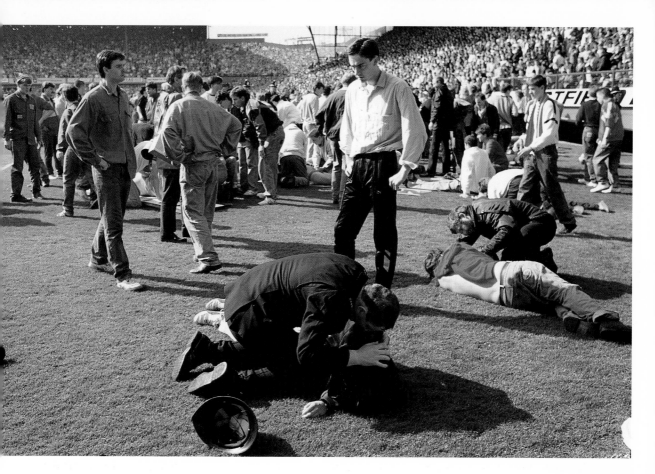

I seemed to pick up a lot in the summer.'

However, things got worse again and Don Hill began to become very irritable, to lose his temper. 'I was a right bastard,' he says. At the end of 1989 he reported the following symptoms: strong feelings of anxiety; extreme short temper; difficulty in concentrating, even for a short time; hatred towards unruly elements; real fear that these feelings would surface and that he would kill somebody. He had nightmares, and Hillsborough would not go away. Six years after the disaster, Hill says:

The anger is not as bad as it was. The main physical feeling is a knot of fear in your stomach. I wake up with it and once it comes it won't go away. It might last for just one day or a week. The other lasting symptom is lack of concentration. My driving sometimes completely goes to pot.

I have convinced myself that when the court case is over, it will all finish. It has to be put to bed now.

Police and others did all they could to revive those hauled unconscious from the crush at Hillsborough, but many were beyond help and were carried on advertising hoardings to a make-shift mortuary.

The scale of the disaster was incomprehensible to the majority of people at the ground, including the police officers. In a few minutes – nobody can say precisely what length of time was fatal for the victims – ninety-five people had been killed, many of them young boys and girls, and another fan died later from his injuries when his life-support machine was switched off.

For many of the witnesses and survivors, the makeshift mortuary in the gymnasium was the worst experience. WPC Jill Thomas had been in the force ten years at the time of Hillsborough, and had just gone back to work after maternity leave. One of her most vivid memories is of the bodies lying on the ground. 'When I saw twenty to twenty-five bodies there before they moved them into the gym, that was the first time I realized the extent of the death toll. I thought they would all get up – it was like they were asleep, like children do in the school hall.'

Jill Thomas is still in the force and has not sought any compensation, but she did suffer afterwards.

All I wanted to do was to get back home and pick up my baby. I had seen so many dead people. My girl did give me something to focus on.

Once I'd seen it on television and the newscaster said it had happened it made it more real to me. I was in a daze before. I was lucky with my baby and I had my husband. I had flashbacks for only a very short period of time, six weeks or so. And tears, uncontrollable anger, particularly when people wanted to talk about it. For about eighteen months, if it ever came out that I was a WPC in Sheffield, people would ask what it was like for all the wrong reasons. I used to let off steam. I used to be rude and swear, it was so macabre. That would result in tears and frustration. After about a year to eighteen months, I was OK.

In the early stages I was drinking more to blot things out. Alcohol is a de-stessing mechanism – it's only when it stops being one that you have to worry. I would have three or four then I'd be OK. I used it. I can't remember everything – you block things out of your mind – but there is no way you could block out Hillsborough.

Afterwards there was a lot of hoo-hah at work about after-effects. One senior officer took the attitude 'You're a police officer, you get on with it,' which made it a bit of a crime to suffer. At the time we weren't up to date, probably. But within the force we are a bit like the ambulance people, we debrief each other. Things have changed in the force since Hillsborough. We did have a welfare department for people whose marriages

broke up and so on, but now it's all changed. I went on a psychological debriefing course and learned how to debrief police officers, and there are now twenty-five of us in the force trained to do that.

Many of the police officers who were at Hillsborough have received counselling of one kind or another. This is not the same as debriefing, which is a chance to talk things over, learn about the probable symptoms of stress, and to understand what might happen to you in the way of psychological reaction.

Debriefing is certainly fashionable, although medical opinion is divided on the question of its real value. Studies abroad comparing those rescue workers who have been debriefed after a disaster and those who have not show little difference in the development of symptoms of trauma. And nearly all research suggests that only a small percentage of people will be either seriously affected or apparently unaffected at all. The most common reaction is to feel seriously upset for quite long periods but to get over it. Among police officers there are sometimes high rates of sick leave in the months following a disaster.

While it is impossible to prove that debriefing helps, it is undoubtedly true that post-traumatic stress disorder, which is a recognizable set of disturbing symptoms, does exist among rescue workers and the degree to which it is likely to take hold will depend on many things, not least the nature of the disaster.

Peter Wells, the former fireman who witnessed Hillsborough as the St John Ambulance duty officer, did not survive his awful experience unscathed.

When I got back home I had to write a report as duty officer and I just sat down and wrote down everything I had witnessed, which maybe got it out of my system. My wife, who was also there with St John Ambulance, did not talk about it much, but she was obviously affected.

The next morning we were due to go to the Crucible in Sheffield for the snooker tournament, and we both said to each other, 'If we don't put our uniforms on again now, maybe we never will.' So we went, but we weren't really there. We told the manager about it and just sat in the coffee bar out of the way.

We all had reactions and on the Tuesday the brigade doctor spoke to us. He had laryngitis and his voice was cracking up a bit, and this set one or two people off. They began to cry and that broke it. I cried as well. Although we did not know it as such then, I suppose we had a kind of debriefing, and that helped.

Only one person has left the brigade because of the Hillsborough experience. Sadly, my wife and I have parted, and I think the experience may have had something to do with it. She has gone her own way and I don't see her now. Since Hillsborough the brigade has set up debriefing sessions for those who might be affected by incidents.

Among the rescue workers at Hillsborough there were many psychological casualties, exactly how many nobody will ever know. These 'hidden' victims have precious little public sympathy because to the supporters, not only did the catastrophe seem to have been caused by those who were supposed to safeguard the crowd's wellbeing, but the rescue operation, such as it was, appeared to be a shambles.

For the ambulance crews the experience was shocking, for they had no chance to save those who died in the pen and were faced with so many dead and injured in the gymnasium. Alan Hopkins, deputy chief of operations with the South Yorkshire Ambulance Service, was outside the ground when the disaster occurred, but saw these harrowing scenes in the gymnasium. He still finds it hard to talk about them.

One thing that got me was that the first person I saw in the mortuary was a seven-year-old kid, and I thought, 'How can someone let a little thing like that come to a football match on his own?' Later I found out that his father was in intensive care. So you get angry with yourself for thinking that. If I have seen that kid once, I have seen him a hundred times.

We were in the triage area in the gymnasium until 4.45pm. When I went home at about 8pm on Saturday night, the first person I saw was one of my grandchildren. Maureen, my wife, has been married to me long enough to let me walk right past and through to the bathroom – I had just left a kid like my grandson lying on the mortuary floor.

We had a function to go to that night but I left after half an hour and went back to Hillsborough. I wanted to retreat, I wouldn't answer the telephone. I was hiding from reality.

Since Hillsborough Alan has suffered a series of problems, including a breakdown.

I am quite happy to identify myself if that will help other people, but a lot of people won't. I have talked to several people who were at Hillsborough and suffered the same things. The infuriating thing about it is that colleagues – police officers – went to court and were told they weren't close enough to claim for stress. I did pursue a claim against South Yorkshire Police and Sheffield City Council. I have recently [December 1995] been advised by the barrister that I am on a hiding to nothing. It's cost me £6,000 of my own money. The ambulance service itself has been quite understanding and helpful, but I don't expect them to fund the case.

After Hillsborough the ambulance people were offered counselling and were interviewed by a consultant in occupational health.

It was to give you the opportunity to talk things through and let them make an assessment. They wanted to see seven to ten people again, but they all refused. I wasn't one of them. Later some went back. It's the macho man thing, the

Some of the police at Hillsborough who threw down their helmets when they went to the rescue sued their own Chief Constable for compensation because of the trauma they suffered.

stupidity of the individual thinking there's nothing wrong.

It was a year after Hillsborough before anyone said to me, 'Get some help.' It was mainly my wife. I went to a doctor in Sheffield and I did all the talking. When I came away and walked down Western Bank, I felt nine foot tall. I had the spring in my step back and I wasn't on anti-depressants. I saw her three times and each time I felt better. Unfortunately she had to go to Scotland, but I recognized that I needed to see somebody. I didn't want anyone from work to know, so I went to my GP. I can't thank him enough.

My job was other people's terror. I needed to carry on working. It was 1994 when I was off, for three months. I was scared to go home and go to bed. Now I sleep like a log, but I'm taking medication. It was a wonderful feeling to put your head on the pillow and have nothing to worry about. It is easy to chuck in the sponge but I had to battle it out. I feel strong as an ox now, but I'm still taking tablets.

The Hillsborough disaster is not over yet, and for many people affected one way or another, it never will be. For the emergency services it was a tragic reminder that in spite of all the planning, training and improvements they have fought for and achieved since the last war, there are still catastrophes which render them powerless. Psychologically, the worst thing they ever have to deal with is a sense of failure, of having been let down by the service they have joined, or of being unable to apply their skills to save lives.

Liverpool fans grieving for those they lost at Hillsborough found their own rituals, creating a memorial of scarves and other mementos to remember the dead.

EPILOGUE

The response of the emergency services to the Hillsborough football disaster is a sobering and tragic episode with which to end this account of the evolution of rescue work in Britain since the Second World War. In so many respects it seemed to represent a spectacular failure for the emergency workers. In fact, the only innovation worthy of consideration at Hillsborough was the willingness of police officers and inspectors to sue for compensation for the mental suffering which the tragedy caused them. There was little or no opportunity on that fateful Saturday for ambulance workers, doctors, firefighters or police to demonstrate the impressive skills they have acquired over the past fifty years.

It is now clear that better safety regulations, rather than better rescue services, would have prevented such a terrible loss of life at Hillsborough. As with most disasters, the cause was human error, for which prevention is a more effective solution than cure. Since the Hillsborough tragedy, the big football grounds have been redesigned so that all spectators are seated and the pens and terraces have disappeared, and ambulance crews attend all major matches.

Hillsborough is a grim reminder that however well prepared rescue workers are, circumstances can confound them. However, there have been other disasters at which the emergency services have been able to demonstrate how far they have come in the last fifty years. There is no doubt that, in that time, the greatest strides in dealing with disasters of various kinds have been made through laws and regulations which seek to prevent them; but despite these preventative measures disasters continue to happen, and did so with a shocking regularity during the 1980s. The tragedies of the 1980s provide an important focus for this book since in that decade the emergency services were called upon to test their accumulated skills again and again, and it was during this time that they established a general procedure for rescue work.

Whether in 1950 or 1990, major accidents invariably throw the emergency services into disarray, at least initially, and present them with uniquely difficult circumstances in which to practise their skills. This has always been an inevitable factor: mistakes were made in the response to disasters as recent as the Clapham rail crash of 1988 and the Kegworth air disaster the following year. Nevertheless, historical comparisons between the major disasters of the 1950s or 1960s and more recent ones of the 1980s do show two dramatic differences in the pattern of rescue work.

The first extraordinary aspect of the evolution of the emergency services is that nearly all the advances of the last fifty years have been instigated by local, and often voluntary, effort. Central government has played practically no part in them at all. Indeed, for twenty years after the war, though the Home Office was prepared to fund a vast structure of civil defence volunteers trained to go into action in the event of a nuclear attack, it would not allow them to go to the rescue in peacetime disasters.

We take for granted now those dedicated and skilled teams of doctors, paramedics and firefighters who work together to save the lives of people trapped in the wreckage of cars (and from time to time of planes and trains). And yet they came into existence in their modern form only as a result of years of tireless and poorly funded campaigning. The story of rescue on the roads, where the relentless toll of crashes and pile-ups over the years has presented the emergency services with both their greatest challenge and their most valuable training ground, is the most telling example of this.

It was an organization of family doctors who were at the forefront of this campaign and who were eventually responsible for setting up the British Association for Immediate Care. They have a very low profile – not many people outside the world of rescue work have even heard of them – and yet BASICS has been the driving force behind the most significant developments in emergency care since the last war. As well as training themselves in immediate care and acquiring new equipment, BASICS doctors campaigned for more sophisticated training for ambulance workers, the result of which is the modern paramedic.

In the early days, BASICS doctors were also instrumental in the drive to arm the fire service with an array of effective extrication gear, gleaned from all over the world. Since it started to take on extrication work at road accidents in the 1960s – which it has continued to do without any statutory obligation – the fire service itself has undergone a revolution. This new responsibility of the fire service has been a far greater innovation than anything that has happened in the techniques of firefighting itself.

The second outstanding change in the last half-century has been the widespread rejection of the old policy of 'scoop and run', whereby priority was given to removing all casualties from the scene of an accident to hospital as soon as possible. In the rush to move the injured without any attempt to categorize the degree of injury or to catalogue the treatment already given, many lives could be lost; now it is recognized that in the first 'golden hour' after injury, the seriously injured can be saved by appropriate medical care on the spot. That means bringing a range of skills to the chaotic and often dangerous scene of a disaster. Here, the emergence of the paramedic has proved to be a vindication of the approach for which BASICS doctors argued for years, as Dr Ken Hines points out:

> *The science of pre-hospital care is evolving steadily. From being very doubtful of the value of on-site care, the academics have done an about-turn. The Royal College of Surgeons in Edinburgh has for the last few years awarded a diploma in pre-hospital medical care to doctors; more recently another certificate,*

> *the PHEC or Pre-hospital Emergency Care course has been welcomed by doctors, nurses and paramedics. A multidisciplinary faculty of pre-hospital care has only this last month [January 1996] been launched by the Royal College. A sound basis for further research and development is now possible. 'Scoop and run' may still have a place in those critical injuries that require immediate life-saving surgery that cannot be performed at the roadside. 'Stay to stablise' is now the normal practice but 'stay and play' is inappropriate. For all the team the ambition is to restore the casualty to their former quality of life.*

But the disagreements about how the emergency services should be organized and operated still continue. Although one or two hospital doctors tried to develop mobile operating theatres and flying squads back in the 1960s, specialist training in the treatment accident victims has remained largely the preserve of GPs working part-time and gleaning expertise from an international exchange of ideas and techniques. Only a handful of hospitals today could claim to have genuine 'flying squads' of doctors trained in immediate care.

These developments in the emergency services could not have been anticipated back in the 1950s. Even today, the history of rescue work is so localised and poorly recorded that few people are aware of the extraordinary way in which it has evolved. This book is an attempt to tell that story through the testimony of those who lived through it and fought for change. It is fair to say that they did so not for any glory – for there was none to be had – but out of compassion and a belief that even in the most terrible of circumstances it might be possible to save lives. If some of these rescue workers suffered in the past from the trauma of what they witnessed, just as many were inspired to find a way of doing better next time.

PICTURE SOURCES